In these pages
you will meet people
from every walk of life:

—the frustrated accountant who threw over his career to build a new one—as a successful artist.

—the doctor who believes the most common cause of death today is suicide—caused by worry, pessimism, and fear.

—the couple who discovered that the promises they made to each other were as important as their promises to others.

—the inventor who was thankful for the deafness that taught him to hear from within. His name was Thomas Edison.

—the nightclub performer whose innocence and faith melted the heart of Al Capone.

—the golf champion who fought his way back from the shadows of death and out onto the links again to inspire millions.

One thing they all have in common:
They tried—and they succeeded! So can you!

P9-DMO-975

OG MANDINO'S TREASURY OF SUCCESS UNLIMITED

EDITED BY
OG MANDINO

PUBLISHED BY POCKET BOOKS NEW YORK

POCKET BOOKS, a division of Simon & Schuster, Inc.
1230 Avenue of the Americas, New York, N.Y. 10020

Published by arrangement with Hawthorn Books, Inc.
Library of Congress Catalog Card Number: 66-15246

ISBN: 0-671-52463-1

First Pocket Books printing March, 1976

19 18 17 16 15 14 13 12 11

POCKET and colophon are registered trademarks
of Simon & Schuster, Inc.

Printed in the U.S.A.

ACKNOWLEDGMENTS

*The editor and the publisher wish to express their thanks to
the following persons for permission to reprint materials in
this book.*

Nova Trimble Ashley for "My White Sheep" © 1965 by
Combined Registry Co.

Dr. Louis Binstock for "Now Is Your Time" © 1966 by
Combined Registry Co.

Dr. Preston Bradley for "You Unlimited" © 1955 by Combined Registry Co.

Curtis W. Casewit for "Victory Over Handicaps!" © 1961 by Combined Registry Co.

N. C. Christensen for "Open That Closed Door—And Sell" © 1965 by Combined Registry Co.

Claire Cox for "Read and Relax for Profit" © 1960 by Combined Registry Co.

Edward R. Dewey for "Cycles . . . And You!" © 1965 by Combined Registry Co.

Cleo Gehrke DuBois for "A New Way to Say Thanks" © 1965 by Combined Registry Co.

Henry N. Ferguson for "Handel's Easter Masterpiece" © 1961 by Combined Registry Co.

R. M. Good for "God Has Been Good to Me" © 1956 by Combined Registry Co.

Peggy Sherman Grinde for "So You're a Salesman" by Bob Grinde © 1965 by Combined Registry Co.

Napoleon Hill for "Your Source of Power" © 1956 by Combined Registry Co.

Jewel Maret Jenkins for "Slip Into Your Neighbor's Shoes" © 1963 by Combined Registry Co.

Lila Lennon for "Danger! Alcoholism Ahead" © 1965 by Combined Registry Co.

Douglas Lurton for "How to Profit From Your Mistakes" © 1955 by Combined Registry Co.

Og Mandino for "Hogan" and "Kelley's Christmas Gift" © 1965 by Combined Registry Co.

Irene McDermott for "How to Appraise Yourself" © 1965 by Combined Registry Co.

Dr. William C. Menninger for "Are You Emotionally Mature?" © 1966 by Combined Registry Co.

Jack Meyer for "How About Your Insomnia?" © 1964 by Combined Registry Co.

Marjorie B. Neagle for "Impact" and "The 'Big Me'" © 1960 by Combined Registry Co.

Bill Nelson for "The Power of Prayer" © 1965 by Combined Registry Co.

Dr. Norman Vincent Peale for "Break the Worry Habit" © 1965 by Combined Registry Co.

Ralph E. Prouty for "Men, It's Okay to Cry!" © 1965 by Combined Registry Co.

Frank L. Remington for "Follow Your Hunches" © 1964 by Combined Registry Co.

William L. Roper for "A Miracle of Positive Thinking" © 1957 by Combined Registry Co.

Frank Rose for "How to Live Longer" © 1965 by Combined Registry Co.

Ed Sainsbury for "How to Rebuild Your Body" © 1960 by Combined Registry Co.

M. Lincoln Schuster for "Assignment: Success" © 1965 by Combined Registry Co.

Harold Sherman for "The Surest Way in the World to Attract Success—or Failure" © 1955 by Combined Registry Co., and for "Turn on Your Magnetic Power" © 1956 by Combined Registry Co.

James C. Spaulding for "Fever!" © 1965 by Combined Registry Co.

W. Clement Stone for "Be Generous!," © 1964 by Combined Registry Co.; "The Man Whose Work Will Never End," © 1957 by Combined Registry Co.; "A Living Philosophy," © 1962 by Combined Registry Co.; "Logic and the Unknown," © 1963 by Combined Registry Co.; "The Letter on Yellow Scratch Paper," © 1962 by Combined Registry Co.; "And They Lived Happily Ever After," © 1961 by Combined Registry Co.; "Get Off the Treadmill!," © 1960 by Combined Registry Co.; "Reminiscing . . . from Newsboy to President," © 1965 by Combined Registry Co.; "Learn to Control Reactions," © 1965 by Combined Registry Co.; and "How to Become a Sales Manager—Now!," © 1965 by Combined Registry Co.

Earl Stowell for "And Then There Was Light" © 1958 by Combined Registry Co.

Edel Sweetland for "A Home for Ten Cents" by Ben Sweetland © 1956 by Combined Registry Co.

Raymond Tetzlaff for "The Luckiest Man Alive" © 1964 by Combined Registry Co.

Duane Valentry for "Can You Afford Your Temper?" © 1959 by Combined Registry Co.

Theodore Vrettos for "Portrait of Courage" © 1964 by Combined Registry Co.

Dr. Harold Blake Walker for "Make the Impossible Your Goal" © 1958 by Combined Registry Co., and for "Thinking Big in Small Places" © 1963 by Combined Registry Co.

Alice Wellman for "Of Whom Shall I Be Afraid?" © 1959 by Combined Registry Co.

Ian Hastings provided the interior art work for the book.

PREFACE

Success is one of the most difficult words in the English language to define. To you it may mean fame and personal power, to another it may be the acquisition of a million dollars, to many it is a happy home filled to capacity with love. Whatever your own personal definition of success may be, you will discover much to ponder in the pages of this book.

Since its first issue in 1954, *Success Unlimited* magazine has been guided by the philosophy, principles and personal efforts of one man—Editor and Publisher W. Clement Stone—and few living Americans write or speak on this subject of success with more authority or experience. His own success story transcends, by far, the heroes of the Horatio Alger stories he read as a young man. Beginning as a newsboy on the streets of Chicago, Mr. Stone applied many of the principles you will find in this book to amass, and share with others, a fortune that is in excess of $160 million!

With such a man at its helm it is inevitable that *Success Unlimited* attracts to its pages nearly every giant in the field of self-help and inspirational writing. The best of their articles which have appeared in the magazine have been chosen for this first *Treasury of Success Unlimited*. You are about to meet people like Norman Vincent Peale, Napoleon Hill, Harold Sherman, Preston Bradley, Ben Sweetland and dozens of others who will show you how to become a whole person—not just wealthy, but also healthy, happy and wise.

Oliver Wendell Holmes once said that many ideas grow better when they are transplanted to another mind. You are about to discover a treasure chest of success ideas. Just one of them could change your entire life. May the ones you transplant from the following pages *to you* grow strong and healthy within your mind and heart until you blossom into the person you've always wanted to become.

OG MANDINO
Executive Editor, *Success Unlimited*

CONTENTS

7 HEALTH UNLIMITED

8 OPPORTUNITY UNLIMITED

9 SALES UNLIMITED

INTRODUCTION

by W. CLEMENT STONE

Editor and Publisher, *Success Unlimited*

Think and Grow Rich by Napoleon Hill was first published in 1937. Millions read it. I did too. It played an important part in motivating me and many thousands who were seeking happiness, health, power and wealth to achieve our objectives. (It is now available from Hawthorn Books, Inc., in a new, instant-aid edition.)

But there were hundreds of thousands of readers who found *Think and Grow Rich* so extremely interesting to read that they were carried away by the stories it contained and therefore did not recognize, study and use the principles that were applicable to themselves. Yes, they were momentarily inspired and undoubtedly benefited to some degree. But after reading the book, they failed to experience the success in life they had the capacity to achieve.

In 1952 I met Napoleon Hill for the first time. Because I had seen the power of *Think and Grow Rich* change the lives of thousands of persons for the better, I encouraged him to come out of retirement and spend five years to complete his life's work. He agreed on one condition . . . that I become his general manager. I accepted because I realized that it is seldom that one man can affect the lives of the masses of his generation for the better, and more seldom, the lives of the masses of future generations.

It is no longer true that if you build the best mousetrap, a path will be beaten to your door. Today the best ideas, services and products must be sold. By vocation I was a salesman and sales manager. I felt that I had a contribution to make in marketing what we subsequently called the PMA (Positive Mental Attitude) concepts.

Principles: Use Them or You Lose Them

During the ten years Napoleon Hill and I were associated, our lectures, books, movies, personal consultations and the magazine *Success Unlimited* developed gratifying, effective, and often amazing results. Through them we inspired and taught individuals how to motivate themselves and others, at will, to acquire the true riches of life as well as monetary wealth and business success. We soon observed, however, that many individuals forgot the principles. They did not learn and employ them well enough to develop them as habits of thought. They lost their inspiration . . . they stopped trying.

We realized that motivation (inspiration to action) is like a fire: the flames will be extinguished unless the fire is refueled. In 1954 vitamins were the rage. We conceived the idea of the monthly magazine *Success Unlimited* to supply regular mental vitamins to revitalize those who were seeking self-help and wished inspiration to keep the flames of their enthusiasm for self-development alive.

So in 1954 Napoleon Hill and I founded *Success Unlimited*. Because of the many requests for an anthology, this book, *A Treasury of Success Unlimited*, was compiled.

Follow a Successful Guide

A Treasury of Success Unlimited can guide you to happiness, good physical and mental health, power and wealth. Like the book *Think and Grow Rich,* each biography, editorial or story is interesting reading. Each contains a message especially for you. Each is designed to stimulate you to develop the unlimited power of your mind.

The many successful authors who themselves use the principles of success revealed in their articles, and who, collectively, have influenced the lives of millions of persons for the better, give you guidelines which you can use to acquire happiness, good health and wealth, and eliminate unnecessary illness and misery.

We do not claim that the anthology in itself will bring happiness, health, power and wealth. But we do know that if you are seeking these, you will generate new ideas and be persistently motivated toward your objectives as you read each chapter. Your life will be changed, for you will be motivated to read inspirational, self-help books which are referred to—books which have already changed countless thousands of lives for the better. You will like the concepts of certain authors and will wish to read their works. In brief, you will recognize new opportunities that were not previously apparent to you. But most of all, when you have a good idea, you will be impelled to follow through with . . . action.

Are You Ready?

Improved good health and happiness can be yours. Wealth . . . you can get it. Power . . . you have it within you. But you must decide whether you are willing to pay the price to extract and use the success principles necessary to acquire these riches of life. The choice is yours, and . . . yours alone.

Perhaps you are ready to discover and use gems of thought—simple universal principles—contained in *A Treasury of Success Unlimited*. Perhaps you are not. If you are not ready, but wish to increase your happiness, physical and mental health, power and wealth, you can prepare yourself *now* by determining specifically what you really want to achieve or acquire. For when you know what your specific objectives are concerning your distant, intermediate and immediate goals, you will be more apt to recognize that which will help you achieve them.

If you have a sincere desire to achieve anything worthwhile in life, an affirmative answer to the following questions will indicate that you are ready to get for yourself the most this book has to offer. Are you willing to pay the price:

> To try to be honest with yourself and recognize your strengths and weaknesses?
>
> To try to engage in self-inspection with regularity?
>
> To try to discover how to develop desirable habits and eliminate those you are convinced are undesirable?
>
> To try to follow the rules revealed to you in this book which you yourself believe will help you to reach your distant, intermediate and immediate goals?
>
> To try to recognize the principles that are applicable to you?

If you are not willing to pay the price . . . if you are not ready . . . then enjoy the book. You'll like it. In all probability your reaction will be such that you will then be ready to reread it and extract the principles that can help you bring your wishes into reality. For each chapter will be thought-provoking as each author endeavors to motivate you to desirable action.

Results Are What Count

In 1952 I made a resolution. I resolved that I would not write an article, write a book or give a speech unless I endeavored to motivate the reader or members of my listening audience to desirable action. I haven't failed to live up to that resolution. This introduction to *A Treasury of Success Unlimited* is no exception. For I am attempting to motivate you to seek and find greater happiness, good mental and physical health, power and wealth, by suggesting you endeavor to recognize, relate, assimilate and use the principles contained in each chapter of this book.

I evaluate my work by the standard: Results are what count. I feel warranted in speaking with authority. The type of material used in this anthology has been instrumental in building Combined Insurance Company of America, of which I am president, into the largest company of its kind in the world. Every sales representative, office employee and shareholder in the Combined Group of Companies (which includes the Combined Insurance Company of America, Combined American Insurance Company, Hearthstone Insurance Company of Massachusetts and First National Casualty Company) has received such information for many years. I have firsthand knowledge of its effectiveness.

Also, as president of the Chicago Boys Club, I have seen the lives of teen-age boys who have been exposed to such inspirational literature changed for the better.

Recidivism has been reduced in prisons where inspirational self-help books and *Success Unlimited* magazine have been furnished to those who were incarcerated, and where they were instructed in the principles contained in this literature.

Letters from many subscribers in the United States and other parts of the world, whom I have not met, indicate the help and inspiration they have received from the magazine.

Therefore, from firsthand experience and testimonials I know that *Success Unlimited* has been a powerful influence in bringing happiness, health, power and wealth to those who had a sincere desire to achieve their specific objectives.

The selected articles from *Success Unlimited* issues of the past, contained in *A Treasury of Success Unlimited,* can do for you what the magazine has done for others.

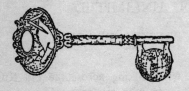

1   YOU
UNLIMITED

Of all knowledge the wise and good
seek most to know themselves.
                      —Shakespeare

Do you believe you have unlimited possibilities for happiness and success? You will, after you read . . .

YOU UNLIMITED

by DR. PRESTON BRADLEY

Many years ago I was walking across the old Rush Street Bridge in Chicago with my coat-collar up and a cap pulled down over my eyes, and I bumped into a man who had on a heavy raincoat and was walking in the opposite direction, with his head down and his hat pulled over his eyes. I said, "I'm sorry, excuse me." He said, "That's quite all right: I want to know if you like the rain, too." I looked into his face and knew him immediately, for it was not many evenings before that I had sat in a theater and had seen him in an interpretation of one of the great classic plays of our literature—the play of Peer Gynt—for the man to whom I was speaking, who became my friend until his death, was the fine, distinguished gentleman, scholar and great actor, Richard Mansfield, who had to struggle and fight to reach that enviable position which he occupied in the American Theater as one of the great interpreters of the classics.

Mr. Mansfield never remembered when he did not want to become a great actor. As a child, like a great many children, he loved to mimic people. His mother opposed him in his ambition very bitterly. She wanted him to go into business and follow the mercantile profession. This was revolting to Mansfield, and he played his first part when he was a lad of seventeen. His

2

mother thought she would humiliate and embarrass him sufficiently so that he never would think of the theater again. At the opening performance of the play, in which he had a very minor part, she and two of her friends engaged seats not far from the front of the stage. When this boy, with his dreams of greatness in the theater—and at its best it is a noble profession, with great social and cultural values—came on in the play, he was publicly ridiculed by his mother. She taunted him! She and her friends laughed, whispered and did everything in the world they could to defeat him. He went through his part, but he said he went to his dressing room and wept bitterly. It seemed that the world had dropped away from him that he should be treated like that, but he said to himself: "I will take my life and develop every bit of it to the perfection of my art. No one can stop me. I believe that I have unlimited possibilities and I will do my best to develop them." Nothing stopped him. Early in life he realized that he was not limited by any influence that could be constructed about him to defeat the highest purposes of his life.

Now, are we all constituted in such a way that our success in life consists of decreasing our limitations? Is it possible for us to have such a clear conception of what those limitations are that we can make it our supreme business to decrease them? Most of us are very poor critics of ourselves. We can easily criticize others and discover what is wrong with them, and we can easily build up an argument for our own side of the situation; but it is a far more difficult thing to be a self-critic—to take the situation that comes into our life and sit down with it frankly and say: "What did I do, or what have I said, that has contributed to this situation?"

There is not a person reading this article who is

living up to his or her own possibilities. If you feel in pretty much of a chaos, frustrated, lots of trouble and worry, just turn the searchlight on yourself and you will discover an available source of power. When you open up the channels and the avenues for that power, it will flood your soul and you will find yourself developing strength and poise, a solidarity, a feeling of security, that nothing on earth can shake!

Is there jealousy in your heart? Is there envy? Opposition? Don't expect a miracle if you retain an obstacle. There is some disciplining you must do. You have got to clear out the old festering sores of your heart. Perhaps you have lied about someone; perhaps you have been unkind; perhaps you have slandered and gossiped. Perhaps you have been "little" when you should have been "big."

How can we transmit our ideals into action so that these ideals can have sway in our lives? Well, we have to begin in our own hearts. When we clear away all that clutters up the channels, the heart and mind are cleansed, the head becomes rarified and the old jealousies, animosities and hatreds are uprooted, and then, though trouble may come in and flood and encompass our lives, there still is a power that reveals our own possibilities. The mere fact that none of us is living up to his best does not predicate that we never can.

Set no barriers for yourself. Admit no barricades or obstacles. Anything in the way? Look at it, examine it, analyze your own relationship to the self-construction of it, clean up your own life and there will be an influx of that power to which there is no limit—unlimited you! You are unlimited! There is no limit for you!

I knew a woman not many years ago who was stricken with polio—infantile paralysis—and as happens so frequently with adults, the resultant paralysis was tragic. One of those well-meaning ladies, you know

the type, came into her sick-room where she was experiencing the tragedy of it, and said to her: "Oh, my
dear, I suppose an illness like this *does* color one's
life, doesn't it?" And this great soul replied, "Yes, it
does color one's life, but I choose the color!"

The trouble is, in this complicated period in which
we are all living, the very atmosphere is charged with
frustration—and assault upon unity and harmony; discord is the theme. We are in chaos. And what is true
of the world society is true of our little individual
world, the one inside us that is so important to us. The
world basically and fundamentally is constituted on
the basis of harmony. Everything works in co-operation
with something else. In the entire world of the physical
universe every law is dovetailed into every other. The
whole cosmic reality is integrated by one harmonic
whole, and whenever discord anywhere comes into
the picture, trouble arises. That is not only true of the
cosmos of which we are a part, but it is also true of
your life and mine in the little orbit in which we live.

How can we develop a technique for the manifesta-
tion of harmony, in spite of the storms around us?
How can we keep our own integration in such operations so that disease and discord and confusion can
never touch a single iota of our own constituency? Is
that possible? Not entirely possible, though it was for
some who have lived: Saint Francis of Assisi, the
immortal and everlasting Gandhi, and I think for
Dr. Albert Schweitzer down in the wilds and jungles
of Africa, and for the classic example of all the history
of humanity—the Master of Men. All the evil that can
be designed against you can be dissipated and erad-
icated by the presence of that divine harmony. There
is strength and beauty in it, nothing fragile or weak. It
is strong; it is unlimited; for beauty is power; truth
has vitality; unity has power. They are the great, posi-

tive, creative, unlimited forces of life. I like in this
connection to think of some lines from a poem of Ella
Wheeler Wilcox:

> You will be what you will be;
>   Let failure find its false
>   content
> In that poor word "environ-
>   ment";
>   But spirit scorns it and is
>   free.
>
> Be not impatient in delay,
>   But wait as one who
>   understands;
> When spirit rises and commands
>   The gods are ready to obey.
>
> The river seeking for the sea
>   Confronts the dam and
>   precipice,
> Yet knows it cannot fail
>   or miss;
>   You will be what you
>   will be!

Have you been selling yourself "short"?
Take a few minutes and learn . . .

HOW TO APPRAISE YOURSELF

by IRENE McDERMOTT

If you are a canny shopper, chances are you evaluate
the merchandise before you buy. But do you do anything about appraising *yourself?* You go through life
selling yourself each day in one way or another—to
the family, to the boss, to the community. And if you
aren't completely happy with any of these relationships, perhaps it is because some of your hidden assets
need to be displayed.

How do you go about doing this? Well, suppose you
were a house. An appraiser would check your foundation, supporting beams, overall square footage, plumb-
ing, wiring and heating plant. Everything has a value—
number of rooms, maintenance of house, and grounds.
Consideration is given to whether the neighborhood is
headed up or down. After he has finished a detailed
report, both buyer and seller can deal intelligently with
full confidence in the property.

Ask yourself whether you are getting the same full
evaluation of your assets and your abilities. Do you
know your true worth? Most of us are unaware of our
possibilities. We envy the solid foundation of the professional man, the impressive facade and substantial
grounds of the businessman, but we cannot relate
ourselves to their success. We are not in their "neighborhood" and our own undeveloped property is in a
state of inertia.

7

If you have such a concept of yourself, it is time you made a survey of your potential. There are aptitude tests that will guide you in searching out your possible talents. There are counselors trained to help people such as you find themselves. If you have access to either, by all means take advantage of it. If not, make your own appraisal. If you owned a piece of rocky, unprepossessing desert land but suspected it contained oil or gold, you would probe to its very depths to find your treasure, wouldn't you?

Only *you* can reclaim the vision you once had, the desire to create and to fulfill yourself. Dreams, you say? Yes, but dreams are the stuff from which all things materialize. First the vision, then the foundation and the outer structure, then the inner refinements, until a satisfactory whole is achieved.

Paul Walters was an accountant with a reasonably secure job, but he hated figures and felt trapped by them. His wife, sensing his dissatisfaction, said, "Let's make a list of things you like to do, and those you do well." His list showed that he:

> *Liked to:*
> fish and hunt
> paint the house
> garden
> putter in wood shop
> do oil painting
> *Disliked:*
> accounting
> selling
> driving a bus
> mechanical work
> *Was good at:*
> accounting
> gardening

shop (fair)
mechanical work

He said, "Looks as if I don't like to work," but the fact was he worked hard at anything he undertook.

His wife asked, "When did you do oil painting?"

"In school. Won a few prizes," he admitted, "but it's silly even to think of taking up art again."

The spark in his eyes told his wife it was not silly. At her insistence he became a Sunday painter. He was never a great artist, but he was so happy and satisfied with his "daubing" that he began to investigate ways in which his talent might also pay. Eventually he found a spot in a commercial art studio. From there he opened a shop of his own.

Today he employs ten people who do silk screen and air brush prints that sell commercially throughout the country. He often gets commissions to do originals for a chain of motels or restaurants. He works happily on these ten or twelve hours a day. His paintings may never hang in a museum, but he is using and enjoying his talent, as well as getting paid for it.

Each of us is endowed with several abilities and talents, with perhaps one predominating. Happy is the man who discovers his hidden gold and is able to utilize it. This is not always easy. Even one with a great desire needs the time to develop his talent to the point where it is practical. This is where his secondary skills will help him.

Paul Walters was not even aware that, with a rather limited talent in art, he had quite a hump of promotional and organizational ability or he never would have made a success of his commercial art venture. He became so fired up with his dream that his other capabilities came to light as needed.

Another young man with a degree in business administration sat in solitary grandeur behind a walnut desk, thoroughly unhappy with his status as a junior executive. He also made a list of his abilities, but he only became more confused than ever.

A job counselor's analysis showed he was a man of simple tastes, enjoyed people and liked challenge. Further study brought out an innate talent for construction or building. The counselor steered this young man into real estate where he was able to buy old houses, remodel and sell them. This satisfied his need for challenge and his contact with people provided the spark which made the *good life*.

When you make your appraisal of self, keep your own counsel, at least at first. Start with the premise that you are a unique individual. No one has quite the same combination of gifts and abilities as you. Make your list as detailed as possible, but make it an honest one. Trying to blow yourself up into a pseudo-likeness of someone you envy or admire will get you nowhere. And certainly being so modest as to underestimate your potential value will not get you out of your present rut.

Study your list thoughtfully, breaking down each item. What prompted you to designate certain ones as being liked or disliked? Did associations affect these decisions? How much experience have you actually had with each? Did you really excel at some of these things, or did you only hope that you might? Were you as bad as you thought at others? Now you are ready to revise your listing again in absolute honesty.

Now—and this is important—which of these would give you the most satisfaction if you could work at it full-time? Since this may change your life, it deserves serious consideration. And don't let your conclusion throw you.

Ken Grady almost did just that. After careful and honest appraisal of his qualifications, he had to admit that he was good at all sports but not at much of anything else. He had played football in college and semi-pro baseball afterwards, and could reel off football scores and batting averages by the yard. He was a tournament golf player, a near-champion swimmer, and never missed a hockey game. You name it, he knew it and loved it. But he was forty years old. It was ridiculous to think of sports as a career now.

Still he desperately wanted to get out of a routine assembly job in an airplane plant. A friend in whom he confided said, "With your knowledge of sports and your voice, Ken, you could be a sportscaster." Ken squelched that with, "Never could talk in front of people."

His friend said, "Take up public speaking, go in for *Toastmasters*."

Ken did, and then went after a niche in radio. He had to settle for a small one, but with further courses in diction his confidence grew and he worked himself up. Today he has quite a respected spot on a major network.

It is never wise to settle on one talent and eliminate other possibilities. Most of us do not have one big, overpowering ability. We are made up of various capacities in varying degrees. The secret is to spotlight one and winnow out others that will fit together to make a whole. If certain required qualifications do not measure up, then go about remodeling them as Ken did.

An appraiser of real property does not look at the front of a house and assess the whole. He checks gutters, downspouts, sprinkling system, topography, and depreciation. Every one of these details is considered in arriving at what is called the "fair market value."

So do not overlook anything that relates to *your* qualifications when figuring your total worth. After you have fitted the pieces together and made a plan for developing your talents, do not hesitate to make changes. Change is the essence of progress. If you have to manage on a reduced income temporarily, remember that the overall outlook is *up*.

You have now discovered your unused wings. You stand in the center of yourself, poised, confident, and in perfect balance—ready to use those wings. This will allow you a new freedom within yourself, and enable you to control the outer aspects of your life to a greater degree than ever before.

Renewed hopes and enthusiasm sparked to action will project you into that forward movement which is the secret of wholeness, happiness and a self-sufficient way of life.

———————————

Even without worldly wealth it's possible for you to . . .

BE GENEROUS!

by W. CLEMENT STONE

Be generous! Give to those whom you love; give to those who love you; give to the fortunate; give to the unfortunate; yes—give especially to those to whom you don't want to give.

Your most precious, valued possessions and your greatest powers are invisible and intangible. No one can take them. You, and you alone, can give them. You will receive abundance for your giving. The more you give—the more you will have!

Give a smile to everyone you meet (smile with your eyes)—and you'll smile and receive smiles . . .

Give a kind word (with a kindly thought behind the word)—you will be kind and receive kind words . . .

Give appreciation (warmth from the heart)—you will appreciate and be appreciated . . .

Give honor, credit and applause (the victor's wreath) —you will be honorable and receive credit and applause . . .

Give time for a worthy cause (with eagerness)— you will be worthy and richly rewarded . . .

Give hope (the magic ingredient for success)—you will have hope and be made hopeful . . .

Give happiness (a most treasured state of mind)— you will be happy and be made happy . . .

Give encouragement (the incentive to action)—you will have courage and be encouraged . . .

Give cheer (the verbal sunshine)—you'll be cheerful and cheered . . .

Give a pleasant response (the neutralizer of irritants) —you will be pleasant and receive pleasant responses . . .

Give good thoughts (nature's character builder)— you will be good and the world will have good thoughts for you . . .

Give prayers (the instrument of miracles) for the godless and the godly—you will be reverent and receive blessings, more than you deserve!

Be generous! Give!

*There are two things you can do when you
make a mistake. You can feel sorry for
yourself and give up or you can learn . . .*

HOW TO PROFIT
FROM YOUR MISTAKES

by DOUGLAS LURTON

So you have made a mistake or many mistakes! So
have we all. But all do not realize that there are intelligent ways as well as stupid ways of confronting
errors. The smart approach is to recognize that it's not
so much the mistakes you have made as what you do
about those mistakes that really counts—on your job,
in a career, in dealing with others at home and else-
where. You can duck and dodge and alibi and mope
and give up trying to eliminate and correct mistakes, or
you can use your head and profit from your own errors
and those of others.

1. You profit by facing mistakes squarely. Don't alibi.
   Man's ego is such that he has an instinctive urge to
alibi failure and rationalize what he does, particularly
when he makes mistakes. That way he loses. He
profits, however, if he intelligently faces up to mistakes,
accepts responsibility, and doesn't hide in a fog of his
alibis. He profits when he refuses to become a fugitive
from the reality of his errors.
   You probably recognize the other fellow's alibis more
clearly than your own. You know the folks who in a
boom blame the inflation, in a depression blame the
season or the weather or the dog or the cat.

Perhaps he who alibis and runs away from his problems may live to alibi another day, but he's not likely to be a winner. You can rationalize yourself into a rut of mediocrity or even into an asylum. You can alibi yourself out of a job or out of promotion. There is a study of why thousands were fired from scores of corporations. More were discharged for sheer carelessness, more for simple failure to cooperate, more for plain unadulterated laziness, than for lack of specific skill on the job. And yet it is safe to say that every one of these thousands of failures had a list of perfect alibis and refused to face up to his or her mistakes.

2. You profit if you don't let mistakes get you down.

The strong men and women bounce back after making mistakes. They have the courage to try to avoid repetition of errors and to improve. The weaklings make mistakes and don't bounce back. They develop fear of trying again and having to make good. They wallow in regrets for past errors. Self-pity is a spoiler. Remorse is a saboteur that can hold you back on any job and in any walk of life.

Babe Ruth whammed out home runs, but also fanned 1330 times and didn't sulk about it. Thomas Edison made countless mistakes in his laboratories. Abraham Lincoln failed in many ventures. The notable inventor Charles F. Kettering would be the last to claim he never made a mistake. But all of these and countless others in more obscure places had one thing in common—they didn't let their mistakes get them down. They recognized that courage has magic in it, and they bounced back after failure and tried again —and won.

3. You profit if you learn how to take criticism.

The first, almost instinctive reaction to criticism is

resentment. Your feelings are hurt! Your ego seems under attack, and an assault on your ego is like a small attack on your life. Many of us resent even our own self-critical thoughts and dismiss them quickly. The multitude resents criticism coming from others and sets up face-saving defenses. But the smart, fully mature man or woman determines to profit from criticism and learns how to take it intelligently.

Adverse criticism may be offered from downright meanness or carelessness; or it may come from a sincere desire to help. Anyone interested in self-advancement should listen to criticism either mean or honestly offered with this in mind: *The more true the criticism may be, the more it may hurt.* Unjust criticism can be rather easily brushed to one side, but if it really stings, the intelligent approach is to seek out the elements of truth that may be involved and take steps to avoid any possible repetition of the criticism.

There is nothing fundamentally new here. It has all been said before and in fewer words by an ancient and wise king named Solomon: "Reprove not thy scorner, lest he hate thee; rebuke a wise man and he will love thee."

4. You profit most by learning from your own mistakes and those of others.

Learning from mistakes is a neat trick that you can acquire if you want to. It is a neat trick because actually we don't necessarily learn much by so-called experience. That may seem to be a challenging statement—and it is. But it is a statement that can be proved easily.

A doctor with fifty years of experience is not necessarily a better doctor than one with ten years of experience. A half-century as a craftsman does not necessarily mean that an individual is better than one with a few years of experience. It all depends on how alert the individual is, how selective he is in piling up his experience.

For instance, "experienced" bricklayers laid bricks for thousands of years in very much the same old way. From generation to generation master bricklayers repeated the methods they had been taught as apprentices. Their instruction included *experience in repeating the mistakes as well as the skills* of their craft. They learned to lay bricks through experience, but they didn't learn from mistakes how to eliminate much lost motion, much of doing it the hard way. It was not until Dr. Frank Gilbreth studied the old "experienced" methods and applied a bit of scientific analysis that experienced bricklayers were taught how to lay many more bricks in much less time and with much less effort.

Unless we learn how to ferret out our mistakes and learn from them, all too many of us may practice our mistakes as assiduously as we practice our successes.

John D. Rockefeller was a master at analyzing his mistakes as well as his successes. Each night Rockefeller set aside ten minutes during which he reviewed and analyzed what he had done during the day. He was critical of all of his actions and judgments and studied them carefully to sort out the mistakes when they occurred, to analyze them, to learn from them.

In his way Rockefeller was using the "scientific" approach to benefit from his mistakes. It is an approach that is used either consciously or unconsciously by all desiring to profit from mistakes and succeed in their occupational and home life and their relations with other people. Here are the steps:

Step one—Determine carefully just what it is you are trying to accomplish and why. What is the job of the moment? What is its purpose?

Step two—What are the pertinent facts involved?

Can you get additional facts bearing on your problem from friends, from reading, from associates and leaders or others in a position to know?

Step three—After considering all of the facts available you should be able to determine various possible courses of action and consider each possible course carefully. Study both its advantages and its disadvantages.

Step four—Narrow down the possible courses of action to the one that comes closest to accomplishing your purpose.

Step five—If you have carefully followed the first four steps and not done a lot of conclusion-jumping, you may be sure that your analysis has given you the one best course of action for you, and the important step is to do something about it, beginning now.

5. You learn by taking courage from the fact that others, even the famous, make mistakes also.

There is a certain measure of comfort for all of us in knowing that there is no man or woman who hasn't made mistakes. No doubt it was this fact that prompted the humorist Mark Twain to point out that *man is the only animal who blushes—or needs to!*

There is rarely a biography or autobiography that doesn't reveal painful and sometimes costly mistakes. Many mistakes are hidden, but many are broadcast to the world. Not long ago an entire book was filled with the boners and bloopers of scores of the most noted radio and television stars—and when you stumble on the air millions know it!

There can be and have been mistakes before the throne and in the seclusion of laboratory or home or factory. Sir Walter Scott, backing away from King George IV of England, sat down hard and smashed a goblet as well as his composure; but his blushes didn't hold him down. Mistakes in full or in part were responsible for certain wallboards, vulcanized rubber, X-rays, aniline colors, photography, dynamite, fiber glass, and many other inventions by people who learned from mistakes.

It is no crime to make mistakes as long as you are trying. It is, however, almost a crime against yourself, at least, to just be around and do nothing. And the gravest mistake of all is to continue practicing mistakes without learning to minimize or eliminate those errors.

It's not the mistakes you make, but what you do about those mistakes that really counts.

Your understanding of the world in which you live will multiply many times when you . . .

SLIP INTO YOUR NEIGHBOR'S SHOES

by JEWEL MARET JENKINS

To the old adage, "If the shoe fits, wear it," might be added some further advice: "Wear it for a bit, even if it does not fit."

Sometimes it takes more than the observations of eye and ear to put ourselves in another's shoes. Plutarch observed this fact long ago when he told the tale of the Roman who had been severely criticized by his friends for divorcing his wife.

The Roman grumbled, "You say, 'Was she not chaste, was she not fair and fruitful?' " Then the Roman held out his shoe to his friends and asked, "Is this shoe not new and well made? Yet none of you can tell where it pinches me." It does indeed take more than the observations of eye and ear to learn another's true circumstance. One must slip into another's emotions as well.

This mental exercise of slipping into another's shoes is not all depressing either. One can *sometimes* learn a lesson in contentment too. All one winter I watched a man who rode the bus to work each morning, carrying his tin lunch pail. One stormy day I thought to myself, "Here is a man trapped by the treadmill if ever there was one."

His eyes were deep set, the mouth stern, and the entire planes of the face as sharp as if carved from granite.

"What has this man to look forward to?" I asked myself. "Obviously he is dressed for hard outdoor labor and probably will eat his cold lunch out in the drifting snow. No wonder his face is set in such stern lines."

Yet there was something else in the face, too, that belied the sternness—some gleam of a deep inner contentment far back in the eyes, some calm acceptance of life's lot that was a mystery to me. One day, during school vacation, the man came on the bus as quietly as before but with a glow of suppressed excitement about him. Holding tightly to his hand and looking up at him adoringly was the most beautiful child I had ever seen. The little girl swept her long auburn curls back from her pink cheeks and said with delight: "Today is the most wonderful day of my life, Daddy, because you are taking me to work with you!"

A smile swept the bus at the little girl's words and suddenly I saw what this man worked for—the hidden treasure that caused the quiet content in his deep-set eyes. And the glow on the little girl's face made the daily grind a little less tiresome for all who rode the bus that morning. We felt we had stepped for a moment into this man's shoes and found that any job may have compensations.

If you are fortunate enough to change jobs occasionally, you can truly put yourself into another's shoes. Try some unfamiliar occupation. Dig a few ditches, saw some logs, scrub a few institutional floors—get the feel of life from such a jobholder's angle. The values that really count may only come home to you from up above the earth, or down in a mine, or from the slant of a hospital bed.

Or you may find yourself doing a mental change of jobs, so that another's problems are brought home to you thus, as happened to a woman of my acquaintance. Jane was a pleasant person, but inclined to be a bit impatient with clerks. She never realized this until the day a customer mistook her for a clerk as she stood near the counter of a large department store. The customer, a large woman whose eyes glittered impatiently behind her steel-rimmed glasses, called out: "Here, you uppity miss. I just want you to know that you've kept me standing here too long. Don't waste your breath on apologies. It's too late for that now. I just want you to know I'm reporting you to the manager for bad service."

Jane gasped at the furiously retreating back of the irate customer. Suddenly, in her mind, were visions of tired salesclerks with aching feet and throbbing heads after a hard day in the store, perhaps with sick children waiting at home; she saw a whole line of clerks she might have subjected to her own imperious shopping demands in the past. Since that day Jane has mentally put herself in the clerk's place wherever she shopped and happier transactions have been the result.

A friend found herself in another's shoes in a deeply emotional way. That summer my friend had spent enough time outdoors to deepen her naturally olive skin to a dusky tan. One day she slipped into a bright red sun dress and went downtown to shop at an elite store. She waited in growing bewilderment while customer after customer who had come in after her was served.

At last she stopped a clerk, asked to see some dresses and went into the dressing room to try them on. The clerk had coldly answered her request to see the merchandise, and it was some time before the dresses came. When they did they were not handed to her. Instead, they were thrown rudely into the booth. Then it was that my friend realized she had been mistaken for a Negro.

Her eyes filled with tears. She felt deeply hurt and as if she had no means to fight back. Then suddenly reason returned to overcome her emotions. She hung the store's merchandise neatly on the hangers, put on her own red sun dress and walked quietly from the store.

This woman has always been especially tolerant—a well-educated person, reaching her opinions in a logical manner. She had thought she understood and sympathized with the problems of minority groups before that day, but her strong emotional reaction to this incident shocked her to a real awareness of another's feelings. She told me: "My feelings for other races and peoples in the minority have been different since that day. I used to *suppose* they had certain attitudes: now I *know* how they feel."

When we can thus truly step for a moment into the shoes of another we are going forward toward better understanding of our fellow men, and a few such steps in strange shoes are worth a thousand strides in our own.

So . . . wear your neighbor's shoes for a while. You

may not like the fit of his shoes—the pinch of poverty, the bruise of ill health, the tight lacings of color or class prejudice—but you will learn things that will surprise you. Trying strange shoes on for size will give you not only the outward appearance of your fellow man, but you will know his inner feelings as well. And you will learn anew the wisdom of that old saying of the Dakota Indians, "I will not talk against my brother until I have walked two miles in his moccasins."

Life will double in enjoyment for you when you finally realize that . . .

NOW IS YOUR TIME

by DR. LOUIS BINSTOCK

No man can be said to be truly happy unless he has attained peace of mind—an inner security—a calm contentment. A man may experience many joys but he is not necessarily happy. He may know many pleasures but he is not necessarily happy. One of the best definitions of happiness that has crossed my reading road is one fashioned by William Henry Channing, Chaplain of the House of Representatives in the middle of the last century: "To live content with small means, to seek elegance rather than luxury and refinement rather than fashion; to be worthy not respectable, and wealthy not rich; to study hard, think quietly, talk gently, act frankly; to listen to the stars and birds, to babes and sages with open heart; to bear all cheerfully, do all bravely, await occasions, hurry never; in a word, to let the spiritual unbidden and unconscious grow up through the common."

The ancient rabbis have put it in this wise: "Who is rich? Only the man who rejoices in his portion, that is, the contented man." Perhaps no better solution has been found than the one discovered by Granpa Tubbs who had been stubborn and crabbed for years. No one in the village could please him. Then, overnight, he changed. Only sweetness and light radiated from his personality. The villagers were astounded. "Granpa," they cried, "what is it that caused you to change so suddenly?" "Well, sir," the old man replied, "I've been striving all my life for a contented mind. It's done no good. So I've just decided to be contented without it."

Some years ago I saw Joe E. Brown in the play *Harvey*. He was the shining star of the production. Afterwards, I had the pleasure of meeting him. I asked him what he liked most about the play. He replied: "The line in which Harvey's drink-happy friend says, 'I always have a wonderful time just where I am, whoever I am with.'" I have thought about that line a great deal and the more I have thought about it, the more I have become convinced that Joe E. Brown was right. The basic lesson we must learn is that you cannot conquer reality by running away from it. You must meet and deal with it wherever it is, whenever it is, however it is, with whomever it is. There is the best place and really the only place where you can find lasting happiness.

Some time ago, while reading the biography of the Dutch painter Vincent Van Gogh, who struggled in poverty and pain all his days and died at too young an age, it would seem, to have reaped a sufficient reward for all his sacrifice and suffering, I ran across a significant passage in a letter to his brother Theo. It reads: "It would not make me so melancholy, Brother, if you had not added something that worries me. You say 'let's hope for better times.' You see, that is one of those things we must be careful of. To hope for better times must not be a feeling but an action in the present. For the very reason that I felt strongly the hope for better times, I threw myself with all my strength into the work of the present without thinking of the future." Van Gogh was not satisfied just to *hope* for better times. He toiled and sweated in order to *make* better times. He lived a short time but he left a glorious heritage to mankind.

Too many of us waste our years waiting for better times in the future or wondering about better times in the past, instead of working for better times in the present. If only we had lived in better times or had been born in better times! If only we lived with better people or belonged to a less underprivileged and despised group! If only we lived in a better home or a better town! If only we had a better business or a better job! If—if—if! Tomorrow—tomorrow—tomorrow! But today is always there; yesterday is gone, and tomorrow may never come. No, now is the time—here is the place. This is the person. This is your home. This is your job. This is your wife—your husband—your child—your mother—your friend. This is your people. This is your country. This is your generation. You can have a wonderful time just where you are, just when you are, just how you are, just with whomever you are.

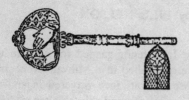

2 FAITH UNLIMITED

All the scholastic scaffolding falls, as a ruined edifice, before one single word—faith.

—*Napoleon*

*Death was minutes away when he dis-
covered . . .*

THE POWER OF PRAYER

by BILL NELSON

The tall handsome Irish tenor gasped for air. He was
only vaguely aware of his bed in a Milwaukee hospital
and the nurse whose anxious face wavered in and out
of his vision. As polio gripped his weakened lungs
more tightly with every labored breath, Marvin Moran
thought desperately of his young wife and two small
children, and of the unpaid mortgage on his home.
This was no time for him to die!

Only a few days before, he had been on a singing
tour in the Midwest—fatigued, but happy that his
career was progressing so well. In the car on his way
home, he developed a fever. It was nothing to worry
about, he thought. But in a few more hours, he was to
learn crushing news: *He had polio*.

"My legs had become immobile," he recalls. "Spinal
polio had done its part. Then bulbar polio started
knocking out the top part of my body. I could feel
the paralysis taking over the nerves in my body as
it moved closer to my head."

Each time that Marvin Moran struggled for one more
painful breath, his stomach cavity went into spasm.
He had reached the crisis. The hush in the room was
broken only by the in-sucking sound that indicated
the approaching end of the singer's life.

"I knew I was dying," Moran said later. "I had been

28

struggling to breathe for a day and a half. I was so
exhausted, I couldn't fight any more."

Then came the most unbelievable moment of his life.
Barely conscious, Moran murmured a simple prayer:

"God forgive me for my sins.

I put my soul in your hands."

Things began to happen—immediately. "As soon
as I let God take over," Moran said, "I felt surrounded
and cradled by warmth. I could sense God's presence.
Suddenly, I had a vision. I saw my vocal teacher of
many years before. He was teaching me how to breathe
properly—using my diaphragm. He was showing me
how to take short 'catch' breaths the way a batter does
just before he hits the ball.

"I stopped gasping so deeply for air and used the
'catch' breath. To my amazement, it began to work.
What a marvelous feeling! I began to breathe fairly
well. The spasms were relieved. I had learned the
secret of *relaxed power*, and it was keeping me alive."

The next two weeks were a living hell. It took
fourteen days for the crisis to pass. But the doctors
were amazed that the polio could go all the way to the
bulb of his brain, then halt so suddenly but a breath
away from death. It was certain now that the Milwaukee vocalist would live.

A grateful Moran told friends: "My recovery from
polio shows the tremendous power of prayer. It is true
that faith can move mountains."

Now a staggering challenge awaited him. He set out
on the laborious, frustratingly slow process of regaining
the use of his semiparalyzed body. The doctors agreed
that he could never walk or sing again.

"But I was convinced that I would," Moran said.
Long, tedious hours of speech and physical therapy
followed. He had to completely rebuild his voice and
his body. In time, he was braced so that he could sit

up in bed. Then he progressed to a wheelchair—and mobility.

"I remember how I'd get into my wheelchair and go behind stage at the Veterans' Rehabilitation Hospital and practice my singing. My voice, nasal from the effects of polio, was awful. But I kept at it."

Only one year after Marvin Moran's battle with death, he limped out to home plate at the Milwaukee County Stadium and sang, "When Irish Eyes Are Smiling." The capacity crowd responded with a thunderous ovation. Then he sang the National Anthem—and 40,000 voices joined him. Although one arm hung motionless at his side, no one noticed; and on that August night in 1954, a new career began for Marvin Moran.

During the next ten years, Moran's melodic voice became a beloved part of the Braves' home games. He sang at the 1955 All-Star game and at both the 1957 and 1958 World Series. More than 14 million spectators heard him perform before he left the club in 1964.

"I loved every moment of it," he says. "Those days will always be happy memories for me."

Today Marvin Moran is a financial planner for the Northwestern Mutual Life Insurance Company. He fills numerous singing engagements, frequently conducting hymn sings throughout Wisconsin on Sunday evenings.

About his experience at the brink of death, Moran says, "God had a special plan for me. I am thankful that He has given me this opportunity to tell people of the wondrous power of prayer."

Her faith withstood even the most terrifying name in the underworld . . .

"OF WHOM SHALL I BE AFRAID?"

by ALICE WELLMAN

It was January of 1931 and my engagement as soloist for Maestro Cherniavsky's Symphony Orchestra at the Saenger Theater, a motion picture palace of New Orleans, would end in two weeks. I loved to sing and for the four-shows-a-day stretch I was paid $125 a week. This was a fortune! This was especially so for a missionary's child reared in the jungles of West Africa, who had earned her musical education and who hadn't owned more than one pair of stockings at a time, until she began to sing for a living six months ago.

But now I was obsessed by worry. Where would my next job come from? The depression was in full sway. In New York City, musical shows were few and seasoned performers were plentiful.

"Alice," yelled the stage manager as I came off stage. "A man's waiting to see you."

The man tipped his black hat and handed me a card which read: "Curly Stone, Booking Cafés and Picture Houses, 54 West Randolph Street, Chicago."

"They need a prima donna in a Chicago club called The Frolics," he said. "They want this girl singer to be a new face in Chicago. I can get you $150 a week."

I was awed by the salary. Of Chicago I knew nothing. I signed the contract and asked, "Who owns The Frolics?"

"Uncle Jakey's the manager." Curly Stone lit a big cigar. "Everybody calls him Uncle Jakey."

"Does he own it, too?"

"I'm personal representative for the club. We'll have a bangup show this turn."

"But whom do I work for?" I persisted.

"What do you care? You'll get good money."

"I have to know before I pay my fare to Chicago. If anything goes wrong, I'll be stranded."

"Well," he grunted, "Uncle Jakey handles the club for Al Brown. You make good with this outfit and you'll be set for life."

On February 15, I opened at The Frolics on Chicago's South Side. It was an elaborate café and I was much impressed, particularly since I'd never even been in a nightclub before.

Three weeks later, I stood in the wings, watching the lineup of girls in exit from their opening number. Their faces shone with vivacity and their gorgeous legs pranced high and fast.

They ran to their dressing room, calling excitedly, "Al Brown's here! Al Brown's out front!"

I heard my entrance music. I was on. My finish song was the sobby torch hit, "Give Me Something to Remember You By." It brought an unexpected ovation. Bowing to the applause, I could see Uncle Jakey at the back of the club, looking at the tables on my left. I looked too.

Around a long table sat a group of perhaps thirty men, pounding their hands together. Blobs of faces, bodies relaxed yet taut. Like the sleepy jungle animals, I thought, ready for a sudden spring.

Three encores later, Uncle Jakey hailed me back

stage. "Al Brown likes your work, kiddo," he said deferentially. "He wants you to come to his table."

"Good," I said. "Maybe he'll order me one of those good steak sandwiches."

We approached the long table. "Which one is Al Brown?" I asked.

Uncle Jakey looked at me questioningly, then pointed out the stocky man at the head of the table. The man's dark hair receded from a high forehead. A great scar cut down the side of his face.

Terror swept over me, buzzed in my ears, blurred my eyes. I had read the papers, seen this man's picture many times. "Al Brown" was his alias.

He rose. The others rose as if on signal. "Where'd such a little girl as you get that big sweet voice?" he rasped, smiling at me.

I couldn't speak but I was praying, silently pleading for help. Then the voice of my mother spoke as clearly as if she stood beside me. "The Lord is the strength of my life; of whom shall I be afraid?"

Al Brown turned to the impassive faces around him. "Meet my friends, babe. This is Nick. Frank. Joe . . . Max . . ." And so on down the line. "You'll join us after the show. We'll go to the hotel for drinks and eats." It was a command.

I wondered at the exact formation in which we walked the short blocks to the hotel. Al Brown and I moved within a solid phalanx of his men. Someone kicked a pebble and the man beside me jerked his hand out from beneath his coat. He had a revolver in it. Well, I was used to firearms. Papa always carried them in Angola because of the snakes and dangerous beasts.

Al Brown's rooms covered an entire floor of the hotel. Luxurious furnishings, refectory tables laden with delectable food, two bars from which liquors flowed into big heavy glasses. A burly man, his gun beside him, fed records into a Victrola.

"Ever had any Napoleon brandy?" Al Brown said to me.

"No," I answered. I'd never heard of it.

He led me into a small room to an elaborately carved table on which sat a dark bottle and two bellied glasses. Proudly, he showed me the label.

"But I don't drink," I said.

He stared unbelievingly at me. "Tell me about yourself, baby," he ordered. "Where were you raised?"

"In Chiyaka on Mount Elende in Angola."

"How'd you come to be there?"

"Mama and Papa took me there when I was six weeks old. They were missionaries. Papa was a doctor and Mama had a school for the Africans."

"Well, you got a new line, anyway," he said skeptically. "Who'd your father doctor?"

"Mostly lepers. But he researched a lot—on serums for snakebites. West Africa has two groups of poisonous snakes, the adders and the cobras. Papa worked on a polyvalent serum that would protect against both types of snakebite."

"Whew! *Nobody* could make that up." He leaned toward me. "I'd have been scared to death. Weren't you?"

"No. But Mama was frightened a lot. She was always protecting us children from mosquitoes and tse-tse flies and scorpions and leopards. We lived in the leopard country. But she didn't let us be afraid."

"What'd she do?" He was curious.

"She always knelt down and prayed."

"So? Your mother still alive?"

"Yes. Mama lives in Wichita, Kansas. We lost Papa but I help my brothers take care of Mama now. She . . ."

Al Brown interrupted me with a kingly gesture. He pinched my cheek with his massive fingers. "Okay, baby," he said, turning to the door.

"Nick!" he roared. Nick, gun in hand, appeared instantly.

"Put this kid in Joe's taxi and tell him to drive her home. Safe."

The next evening, when I reached the club, Uncle Jakey handed me a small box from a well-known florist.

"For you, Alice," he said respectfully. The box held a corsage of three white orchids. I laughed delightedly for they were the first ones I'd ever received in a box. In the African rain forest, they grew on trees. Their centers were pushed open. Each held a folded hundred-dollar bill.

"Al Brown told me to deliver them to you personal," he said. "A message goes with them. The orchids are for you but the money's for your mother."

That night I wrote to my brother Paul. Paul was on the Kansas City *Star* and I thought he'd find the facts of mother's gifts amusing.

Two days later, Paul rapped on my hotel room door. "You're leaving Chicago," he said.

"But Paul, my contract—my salary?"

"Hurry and pack, honey," he said firmly. He put me on a plane that evening. Back in New York, I landed a job in an operetta, *not* a nightclub.

Since I sang in The Frolics twenty-eight years ago, I have seen Al Brown's name blazoned in headlines many times. I know there was one moment in his life, though he may never have recognized it, when he felt the power of prayer. And that was the moment when I learned the strength that came from the Lord, whether you faced the dangers of African jungles or worked for Al Capone in Chicago.

Henry J. Kaiser's wealth is great but he learned the true values of life from his mother . . .

THE MAN WHOSE WORK WILL NEVER END

by W. CLEMENT STONE

I went to Hawaii for several reasons, one of which was to find true stories. I found one that had a terrific impact upon my future development—one that could also change the entire course of *your* life if you are ready.

It concerns the "common horse sense philosophy" of a man close to the top of the list of America's ten living men whose lives have been most beneficial to their country during peace and war, and who have generated great constructive forces to inspire men and women of future generations, *the man whose work will never end*—Henry J. Kaiser.

You know him by name—your future success would be assured if you could relate and assimilate into your own life his fundamentally effective philosophy. He continually proves that it works for *anyone who uses it*. He would like to share it with *you*. Regardless of your age, *you* can employ his formulas for success.

Today the wealth of the companies identified with his name have total assets of approximately one billion dollars—30 active corporations consisting of 125 plants in 20 countries which turn out over 300 products.

THE HAWAIIAN VILLAGE

I found my inspiring story there. The Hawaiian Village is the tourist's, artist's, philosopher's and author's dream come true of everything that Hawaii is and ought to be; Hawaiian music, singers, beautiful dancers; a white sand beach, six swimming pools and a lagoon; a yacht harbor with its catamarans and skiing facilities: palm-thatched guest houses, clusters of Waikiki Beach lanais, a 14-story hotel (the construction of additional hotels will ultimately accommodate four thousand guests at one time) in a Polynesian setting of acres of fragrant tropical gardens and palm trees where birds sing happily—all under a bright tanning sun during the day. Yet the dry air is cool in the shade; there is a covering of myriads of bright stars at night; and there is a monument to the needy in the form of a proposed ultramodern hospital. There are facilities for conventions in the unique aluminum dome auditorium with a seating capacity of eighteen hundred persons.

More importantly, at the Hawaiian Village you feel that the brotherhood of man is a reality and not a theory. Europeans, Americans, Polynesians and Orientals meet on a plane of equality. They like and respect each other. There is magic in the air. Catholic and Protestant church services are held in the same church building, which is designed in the style of a native chief's longhouse.

A Hawaiian said to me, "Henry J. Kaiser inspires us. He has done more for Hawaii than anyone in our lifetime. He gives the young generation hope and courage. There was a time when no one dared compete with the 'Big 5' which had controlled these islands for generations. Henry J. Kaiser had the courage—he succeeded."

APPLIED IMAGINATION

In Henry J. Kaiser's workshop Robert C. Elliott, his executive assistant, said, "He first pictures in his mind what he wants; he tells one of our artists; the artist draws the picture; our architects lay out the plans; a date is set for construction; the work is completed. See for yourself. Here are the original pictures of the buildings in the Hawaiian Village; here are the photographs of the finished construction." Yes, Henry J. Kaiser uses applied imagination.

A SELF-EDUCATED MAN

Henry John Kaiser was born May 9, 1882 in Sprout Brook, New York, one of four children of Francis John Kaiser, a mechanic in a shoe factory, and Mary (Yopps) Kaiser, a practical nurse, both of whom were German immigrants.

At the age of thirteen he discontinued school and trudged the sidewalks of New York, week after week, looking for work. He has always been inquisitive—he wanted to learn. Like Thomas A. Edison, Andrew Carnegie and other self-made men he continued to learn after leaving school. He learned from experience —as a young salesman and a sales manager (perhaps the greatest vocation for any person interested in learning about people and interested in self-improvement) and he learned from history, literature, poetry and religious sermons. He eagerly listens to the messages that are applicable to him!

For example, at the age of sixteen he was impressed by a sermon, the essence of which was "Cherish the rich memories of the smiles and sunshine you have given to others and the friendly smiles and sunshine that others have given to you." At the age of nineteen, when he became an independent businessman, he put up a sign the size of a billboard over his store which read, "Meet the Man With a Smile."

He reacts to such inspirational writings as these:

"Ah, but a man's reach should exceed his grasp, or what's a Heaven for?"

"All things are possible to him who has faith. Because faith sees and recognizes the power that means accomplishment. Faith looks beyond all boundaries. It transcends all limitations. It penetrates all obstacles. And it sees the goal. Faith never fails. It is a miracle worker."

"If thou canst believe, all things are possible to him that believeth."

" 'Tis the hardest thing in the world to give everything, even though 'tis usually the only way to get everything."

"What! Giving again? I ask in dismay, and must I keep giving and giving away? 'Oh no,' said the angel looking me through, 'just keep giving till the Master stops giving to you.' "

NEVER GROW OLD

I predict that Henry J. Kaiser will live to celebrate more than his hundredth birthday. He himself says, "There are those who *never* grow old in mind and spirit and interest. How is it possible never to grow old, *really* old? By keeping young in all thinking, young in imagination, fresh in spirit, heart and soul. It *can* be accomplished!

"Mother used to say, 'Henry, be sure *you* practice what *you* preach.' " He does! He says, "Work! Put your life's plan into determined action and go after what you want with all that's in you!" He discovered from experience, "The person who makes fun and joy out of his work can leap out of bed at dawn and work with zeal; work becomes a habit."

Never grow old! At the age of forty-five, Henry J. Kaiser engaged in the $20 million project of building two hundred miles of highway with five hundred bridges in the interior of Cuba. It meant organizing six thousand workers and fighting serious obstacles. It was this vast project that crystallized his idea to employ the principle of the mastermind alliance. He shared this enterprise with other contractors through partnerships and associations; thus he developed the strength of combined knowledge, skill, capital and manpower. This principle is a most important ingredient in his formula for effectively building mammoth constructions with speed.

Kaiser's experience in Cuba made it easy for him to organize six large firms into a cooperative enterprise known as Six Companies, Incorporated. He became chairman of the executive committee. Through his guidance and experience were built the Hoover, Bonneville, Grand Coulee and Shasta Dams, the piers of the San Francisco Bay Bridge, levees on the Mississippi River, and pipelines throughout the Northwest, Southwest and in Mexico. At the age of fifty-seven, he founded the largest cement plant in the West, which was the second largest in the world.

Keep in mind that throughout his life when others said to him as they have to you, "It can't be done" he knocked out the "t" and said to himself, "It can be done!" And he did it.

Yes, never grow old. At about the age of sixty, during World War II, he built over one thousand five hundred ships with such rapidity that he startled the industry. He dared to think of new, fast methods to get results. He founded the first (and still the only) iron and steel plant on the Pacific Coast at Fontana,

California. He built and operated two magnesium plants. He supplied all of the bulk cement used in the construction of our Pacific fortifications. He operated plants manufacturing aircraft parts, and he managed the largest artillery shell operations in the country.

THE MOST PRICELESS GIFT

Henry J. Kaiser inherited from his mother "the most priceless gift"—an inheritance that you or any father or mother might pray to give to your children. When Mary Kaiser was in her late thirties, after her day's work, she spent hours as a voluntary nurse helping the unfortunate. Often she said to her son, "Henry, nothing is ever accomplished without work. If I leave you nothing else but the *will to work,* I leave you *the most priceless gift*—the joy of work!"

"LOVE PEOPLE AND SERVE THEM"

"It was my mother," continued Mr. Kaiser, "who first taught me some of the greatest values in life—love of people and the importance of serving others. Mother was only forty-nine and I was sixteen when she died in my arms—died because of lack of medical care. The thought of my mother, or your mother or father, or children or loved ones dying prematurely when a doctor or a good hospital could save them—the thought of such needless sacrifice of human lives has always prodded me into action."

Hundreds of thousands of persons have received medical, surgical and hospital care at low cost. Others who suffered a speech paralysis can now talk. The crippled have been restored to useful lives in rehabilitation centers. All this has happened because of the inspiration of a mother who died in the arms of her son because she was too proud to ask for charity and too poor to pay for medical care—a mother who said to her son, "Love people and serve them." The Kaiser Foundation—a nonprofit charitable trust—is only one of the monuments to her memory.

HUMAN RELATIONS

Henry J. Kaiser knows how to get along with people. Many feel that he has a genius for developing good relations with labor unions. He says, "The great truths by which to live are simple. The Sermon on the Mount and the Golden Rule are simple. I always try to stress the positive approach—down-to-earth attitudes that can succeed. Here are some of them:

"First—mutual acceptance, recognition and confidence in each other; secondly—honesty and integrity in our dealings together; thirdly—in bargaining, we must understand each other, not bog down in doubletalk or demand lopsided victories."

PRAYER

In each of Henry J. Kaiser's speeches he utters a prayer. *(You may obtain copies of his speeches by writing to: Public Relations, Kaiser Building, Oakland 12, California.)* In the sincerity and spirit of the Man Whose Work Will Never End this article closes with a reverent prayer that Henry J. Kaiser will continue to live for many years and thus add additional momentum to the good work he has so ably started.

HOW TO BECOME THE PERSON YOU WANT TO BE

Henry J. Kaiser says:

1. "Know yourself and decide what you want most of all to make out of your life. Then write down your goals and a plan to reach them.

2. "Use the great powers you can tap through faith
   in God and the hidden energies of your soul
   and subconscious mind.

3. "Love people and serve them.

4. "Develop your positive traits of character and
   personality.

5. "Work! Put your life's plan into determined
   action and go after what you want with all that's
   in you."

------

*Each man weighs his gifts from God on a
different scale . . .*

"GOD HAS BEEN GOOD TO ME"

by R. M. GOOD

For 25 years I watched him fight cancer of the face.
First, just a small speck that began to grow larger;
then, year after year, I watched him go to the hospital
and have a bit more cut out each time. As the years
went by, his face was hardly a face at all as more and
more was cut away. But always when he returned, with
what was left of that face, he tried to smile and never
once uttered a complaint or seemed to be downhearted.

He was a skilled mechanic and finished carpenter—
recognized as the best in all the surrounding Ozark
hills.

When he did a job he seemed to stand back and
survey it to see if there was anything left out that
could be added to make it as nearly perfect as possible.
Then he would see some little place that the average

person would pass up and he would be busy touching up this and that. Then, when he had done his best again, he would look it over and a smile of content-ment would come over his face.

I suspect he often said to himself, "My work will be my face and my life." I doubt if he often looked in the mirror and noticed that damaged face where each day the cancer bit a mite deeper.

No matter how humble the home he worked in, or how small the job, or how crude the other work around and about, it never seemed to bother him at all. This was his work, and it had to be done right. He appeared never to give a glance at the work of others; a shoddy job done by someone else was not his concern. His own work seemed to be all that mattered. Nevertheless, I suspect when the job was done he had an inner sense of pride and joy when he saw how outstanding it was —but never once did I hear him boast about it.

As the years went by, he became weaker and weak-er, his step was less sure, and his hands did not move with the confidence and speed that had so character-ized him. He was unable to do many things he had done before. However, no matter what the work or pay, he always had an insatiable desire to do a good job.

The help he was able to get was not able to catch his vision; they thought he was cranky to try so hard to complete each and every detail. So more and more he worked alone. He did not complain or bitterly rail at the inefficiency of the other fellow. He would just appear the next morning by himself with no explana-tion of the absence of his helper.

During the latter days when he had only the sham-bles of a face, he would wrap it up in a red bandana handkerchief, leaving only his eyes showing.

When you met him on the street, there was always a

cheery greeting. As time went on and he found it more and more difficult to say the words, often his greeting would be given with a move of his walking stick. This stick, too, was a thing of beauty, carved out by his skillful hands.

His life seemed to be filled with contentment and peace. I am sure many times he thanked God for those hands and for the fact that they were marred in no way.

He often would be missed about his usual haunts for weeks, or perhaps months, as he would make his journey to the hospital for the surgeon to cut away a little more. Then you would see him again—a bit more gruesome. There would be no complaint, no telling of his operation and the pain. He would just quietly go about the work that was always awaiting his return.

In all of this quarter of a century, I never knew him to come back with any complaints or mention in any way the pain. You would think there was nothing the matter if you did not see his face.

When his days of labor seemed to be coming to an end, his chief concern was that his tools might be in good hands. He sent for me one day and told me that he wished I would find for him some young man who would appreciate and properly use them.

When I took a young man to see him about the tools, there came over his face a look of contentment and satisfaction. His work was finished and he was ready to cash in.

A few days before he died I went to see him. He was walking in the yard. His face was nearly completely covered with bandages and only his eyes were uncovered. As he hobbled about the yard, he said to me, "I am going to keep young just as long as I can."

The day he died I went to see him again. The odor

in the room was so offensive you could hardly stay there. What was left of his face was a mass of scars and there was really no longer anything to cut away. You could tell he was in great pain and had many a sleepless night, but still there was no word of complaint.

I shall never forget his last words. Ever afterwards they have made me ashamed whenever I am inclined to complain. Still, day after day, they are vivid in my memory.

These words were: "God has been awfully good to me. I have never had any reason to complain."

Poverty-stricken, paralyzed and rejected he still presented the world with the greatest oratorio ever written—The Messiah . . .

HANDEL'S EASTER MASTERPIECE

by HENRY N. FERGUSON

On a cold winter night in 1741, an elderly, stoop-shouldered man ambled listlessly along a dark London street. George Frederick Handel was starting one of the aimless, despondent wanderings which had become a nightly ritual with him. As he walked, his tortured mind flitted between the memories of past glories and the hopeless despair of the future. For four decades Handel had written music which had won him the adulation of the aristocracy of England and the Continent. The favorite of royalty, he had been showered with many honors. And then, abruptly, court society had turned on him. His once-famous operas were broken up by gangs of rowdies. It was only a matter of time until Handel was reduced to abject poverty.

A cerebral hemorrhage paralyzed his right side. He was unable to walk, move his right hand or write a note. Doctors could give him no hope for recovery.

The old composer went to Aix-la-Chapelle to take the baths. In spite of his doctor's warning that staying in the scalding waters longer than three hours at a time might kill him, Handel stayed in nine hours at a stretch. Gradually inert muscles took on new life. He began to walk, his hand lost its paralysis.

As his health returned, Handel began working again. In a frenzy of creativeness, he wrote four operas in quick succession. Again he found himself the recipient of many honors. And again the hand of fate struck him a cruel blow.

Queen Caroline, who had long been his patroness, died. Handel's income was immediately reduced. England found herself in the grip of such a bitter winter that fuel could not be wasted on heating the theaters. All engagements were canceled. Handel lived for a while on money borrowed from friends. As he sank deeper into debt, he lost his creative spark. He felt old, tired and hopelessly beaten.

On this night, as he tramped restlessly along a deserted street, he paused for a moment before the dark outline of a church. In bitter self-pity he pondered his situation. Why had God permitted his creativeness to be restored, only to let it be torn once more from his grasp?

Head bent against the sting of an icy wind, he made his way back to his humble room. As he pushed open the door he saw a package lying on the table. Tearing off the wrappings, he saw that it was the text of a musical composition. It was entitled *A Sacred Oratorio*.

Handel grunted contemptuously when he saw that it was from a second-rate poet, Charles Jennens. The note asked if Handel would start work immediately on the oratorio. A postscript added the information that "the Lord gave the Word."

Handel leafed indifferently through the oratorio. Suddenly a passage held his eye: "He was despised and rejected of men. . . . He looked for someone to have pity on Him, but there was no man; neither found He any to comfort Him."

A sense of kinship warmed Handel's heart. He read on. "He trusted in God . . . God did not leave His soul in Hell . . . He will give you rest."

The words, burning into his consciousness, began to take on meaning. "I know that my Redeemer liveth . . . Rejoice . . . Hallelujah."

The old fire that had inspired the rulers of Europe began to rekindle. Wondrous melodies bubbled up from the seething caldron of his mind. He grabbed a pen from the table and started writing. With unbelievable swiftness his notes filled page after page.

His manservant found him the next morning, still bent over his makeshift desk, still writing. Noiselessly he put down the breakfast tray and slipped quietly away. When he returned at noon, the tray had not been touched.

For days the old servant watched anxiously over his master. Handel refused food. He wrote continuously. Sometimes he would pause, striding up and down, flailing the air with his arms. When he finished the triumphant climax to the "Hallelujah Chorus," tears were streaming down his cheeks. "I did think I did see all Heaven before me and the great God Himself!" he told his servant.

Handel labored like a man possessed for 23 days. Then he collapsed on his bed, exhausted, and slept for

17 hours. On his desk lay the score of the greatest oratorio ever written—*The Messiah*.

Really worried now, Handel's servant sent for the doctor. But before the physician arrived, the composer was sitting up, yelling for food. He eased his hunger pangs by wolfing half a ham, washing it down with tankards of ale. Then he lit his pipe and joked with his amazed doctor.

Although Handel was sure he had composed a masterpiece, London wanted no part of it and so he took *The Messiah* to Ireland at the personal invitation of the Lord Lieutenant. Handel insisted that the proceeds of its performance must go to charity.

Arriving in Dublin, Handel lost no time merging two choirs and beginning rehearsals. So many tickets were sold for the first performance that notices were published in the newspapers begging the ladies not to wear their hoopskirts to the concert and the men to leave their swords at home. On April 13, 1742, crowds waited at the theater doors for hours before the opening. The response was tumultuous—even Handel was awestruck by his creation.

After his Dublin triumph, London began begging to hear the work. It was during the first London performance that a strange thing happened. The audience, carried away by the power of the "Hallelujah Chorus" and following the King's example, arose in unison as though by a prearranged signal. Since then audiences the world over have expressed a similar respect by rising at the onset of this chorus and remaining standing until its conclusion.

For the remainder of Handel's life he presented *The Messiah* annually. All the proceeds went to the Foundling Hospital, and in his will he bequeathed the royalties from this work to the same charity.

Handel once more ran the gamut of misfortune, but

never again did he permit despair to get the upper hand. Age robbed him of his vitality. He went blind, but his unflagging spirit never wavered.

On the evening of April 6, 1759—Handel was 74—he attended a performance of *The Messiah*. Suddenly he collapsed. He was taken home and put to bed. His spirit was still valiant, but the flesh was beginning to weaken. "I should like to die on Good Friday," he announced to his friends. And on April 13, the anniversary of the first presentation of *The Messiah*, in accord with his wish, the great composer's soul left his body forever.

For two hundred years now his spirit has gone marching on in *The Messiah*—an international symbol of the triumph of hope over despair. For the genius of his pen lighted a torch that has brought illumination to the dark places of the earth wherever there are voices to sing and hearts that beat with courage.

You have an "unseen partner" who will help you . . .

BREAK THE WORRY HABIT

by DR. NORMAN VINCENT PEALE

Nobody does good work who tugs and strains and is rigid about it. "Easy does it" is the proper method.

The person who works the easiest does the most in the shortest time and his work shows the mark of skill. Don't live and work the hard way. We suggest that you

study and master the following rules for making your
work easy.

1. Drop the idea that you are Atlas carrying the
world on your shoulders. The world would go on even
without *you*. Don't take yourself so seriously.

2. Tell yourself that you like your work. It may be
difficult to make yourself believe that, for you may
have talked yourself into hating it. Or you may be a
"fighter of the job," that is to say, you struggle against
it rather than with it. This emphasis on liking your
job will tend to make it a pleasure instead of a drudg-
ery. Perhaps you do not need to change your job.
Change yourself and your work will seem different.

3. Plan your work for today and every day, then
work your plan. Lack of system produces that "I'm
swamped" feeling. To arrange work in an orderly way,
and perform it in the same manner, makes the total
job infinitely easier.

4. Decide that you will not try to do everything at
once. That is why time is spread out. Repeat the wise
advice from the Bible, "This *one* thing I do." Say
that to yourself *now*, three times, emphasizing the
word *one*. One step at a time will get you there much
more surely than haphazardly leaping and jumping. It
is the steady pace, the consistent speed that leads most
efficiently from start to destination.

5. Practice becoming expert in correct mental attitudes, remembering that ease or difficulty in your work
depends upon *how* you think about it. Think it is hard,
and it is hard. Think it is easy, and it is easy. So spend
a minute now in thinking of your work as easy.

6. Determine now to restudy your job for "Knowledge is power" (over your job). It is always easier
to do a thing right. Make your own job analysis to
discover more right ways of doing things. The right

way is right because it meets less resistance and is therefore easier than the wrong way.

7. Practice being relaxed about your work. Again remind yourself that "Easy always does it." Do not press or strain. Take your work in your stride. One way to do this is to repeat such a work formula as the following: "I can handle this job. I know this material or this business. I am well informed about it and am competent to deal with it; therefore, I will have no fear or nervousness about it and besides, God is with me to help me." This will give you a feeling of peace and confidence and you can do the job in a relaxed frame of mind.

8. Discipline yourself not to put off until tomorrow what you can do today. Accumulations make the job harder than it actually is or should be. Do not drag yesterday's burdens along with you. Keep your work up to schedule. Spend a minute *now* listing the things to do today, and tomorrow, and the next day. This will immediately relieve today's burden, for usually you do not need to do so much right now as you nervously think you do. If your mind gets the idea that you have too much to do, it immediately accepts tired thoughts, your energy drops, and the job becomes heavy and hard.

9. Pray about your work, today's work. You will get some of your best ideas that way. Never start a day or any job without praying about it.

10. Take on the "unseen partner." It is surprising the load He will take off you. God is as much at home in offices, factories, shops, as in churches. Do not spurn God's help, for He has broad shoulders and strong arms and wonderful ideas. All are available to you. He knows more about your business than you do. His help will make your work easy.

(If this article helped you, you can obtain a free copy of Dr. Peale's *Self-Improvement Handbook* by writing to Department SU, Foundation for Christian Living, Pawling, New York 12564.)

A bright light guides your ·path to success when you adopt . . .

A LIVING PHILOSOPHY

by W. CLEMENT STONE

The essence of a living philosophy is that it must be alive. To be alive, it must be lived. To be lived, you must act! Actions, not mere words, determine the validity of a man's living philosophy.

For faith without works is dead.

Whether he recognizes it or not, everyone has a philosophy. You become what you think. Now my living philosophy is:

First, God is always a good God.

Secondly, truth will always be truth, regardless of lack of understanding, disbelief or ignorance.

Thirdly, man is the product of his heredity, environment, physical body, conscious and subconscious mind, experience and particular position and direction in time and space . . . and something more, including powers known and unknown. He has the power to affect, use, control or harmonize with all of them.

Fourthly, man was created in the image of God, and has the God-given ability to direct his thoughts, control his emotions and ordain his destiny.

Fifthly, Christianity is a dynamic, living, growing experience. Its universal principles are simple and enduring. For example, the Golden Rule, "Do unto others as you would have others do unto you," is simple in its concepts and enduring and universal in its application. But it must be applied to become alive.

Sixthly, I believe in prayer and the miraculous power of prayer.

Now what does this philosophy mean to me? It wouldn't mean a thing unless I lived it. To live it I must apply it. And therefore I shall give you an illustration of how I apply it in a time of need. Then it may be more meaningful to you.

In 1939 I owned an insurance agency which represented a large Eastern accident and health insurance company. Over a thousand full-time licensed agents were operating under my supervision in every state in the United States. My contract was verbal and provided for exclusive distribution of a specified series of accident policies. Under this working agreement, the business was owned by me. The company printed the policies and paid the claims. I assumed all other expenses.

It was spring. My family and I were vacationing in Florida when I received a letter from one of the chief executive officers of the company. This letter was brief: It stated that my services would be terminated at the end of two weeks; my license to represent the company, and the licenses of all my representatives, would be cancelled on that date; no policies could be sold or renewed after that date; and the president of the company was leaving on a trip and couldn't be reached for two months.

I was faced with a serious problem. The type of contract I had just wasn't being made any more. A new connection for a national operation such as mine within two weeks was an improbability. The families of the one thousand representatives who worked for me would also have a problem if I didn't find a solution.

Now what do you do when you have a serious personal problem—a physical, mental, moral, spiritual, family, social or business problem?

What do you do when the walls cave in?

What do you do when there is no place to turn?

That's the time your faith is tested. For faith is mere daydreaming unless applied. While true faith is applied continuously, it is tested at the time of your greatest need.

Now what would you have done if you had been faced with my problem? Here's what I did:

I told no one, but cloistered myself in my bedroom for 45 minutes. There I reasoned that God is always a good God; right is right; and with every disadvantage there is a greater advantage if one seeks and finds it.

Then I kneeled down and thanked God for my blessings: a healthy body, a healthy mind, a wonderful wife and children, the privilege of living in this great land of freedom and unlimited opportunity, and the joy of being alive. I prayed for guidance. I prayed for help. And I believed that I would receive them.

And I did get into positive mental action!

On arising I began to engage in thinking time. Four resolutions were made:

1. I wouldn't be fired.
2. I would organize my own accident and health company and by 1956 would have the largest company of this kind in the United States.
3. By 1956 a specific objective would be reached. It was of such magnitude and so personal that it would be improper to mention it here; and
4. I would reach the president of the company

regardless of what part of the world he might be in.

And then I got into physical action. I left the house and drove to the nearest public telephone booth to try to talk to the company president. I succeeded because I tried. The president was a kindly, understanding man of principle. He gave me permission to continue operations upon my agreement to withdraw from the state of Texas where the general agents of the company were having some competitive difficulties with my representatives. We were to meet at the home office in 90 days.

We did meet in 90 days. I am still licensed for that company and continue to give it business.

When 1956 came, the company I organized in 1939 was not the largest accident and health company in the United States. But it was the world's largest stock company writing accident and health insurance exclusively. My specific personal objective had also been achieved.

Now, what do you do when you have a serious personal problem—a physical, mental, moral, spiritual, family, social or business problem? Your philosophy will determine your answer.

Remember: The essence of a living philosophy is that it must be alive. To be alive, it must be lived. To be lived, you must act! Actions, not mere words, determine the validity of a man's living philosophy.

3 IDEAS UNLIMITED

Ideas control the world.
— *James A. Garfield*

Just a simple magnet and some iron filings may give you the idea and motivation you need to ...

TURN ON YOUR MAGNETIC POWER

by HAROLD SHERMAN

Did you ever experiment with a magnet and iron filings? A magnet has the power of attraction; the filings have magnetic properties which respond when brought in contact with a magnetic field.

First, you hold the magnet just far enough away from the pile of iron filings so that its "magnetic pull" doesn't reach them. Nothing happens.

Then you move the magnet a little closer. You see little wisps of the filings around the edges begin to pull away from the pile and adhere to the end of the magnet, moving across the charged space.

Now you thrust the magnet forward so that the entire pile of iron filings comes within its field—and there is an instantaneous mass movement of the magnetized particles to cluster about the poles.

You have control of this operation. You can remove the iron filings, replace them on the table and approach them with the magnet from any direction you decide—and they will be drawn to you just as surely and speedily.

If, however, you decide *not* to use the magnet; if, with all its power to attract, you let it lie idle, the iron filings remain undisturbed. To look at them, you would not know they had any capacity to respond to magnetic attraction. They would appear as an inert mass, utterly incapable of any movement.

Now, for sake of illustration, imagine this pile of iron filings as the opportunities you need to attain what you desire in life. These iron filings are at present beyond your reach; they may not even be in sight; they exist, for the moment, in your future.

The only way you can attract these opportunities to you is through the magnetic power in your own mind. The power is there, just as it exists in a physical magnet, but it doesn't function automatically. You have to control and direct this power.

You have to do it by first deciding in what direction you want to go—then pointing your mind in that direction, as you would a magnet. Picture your objective clearly in your consciousness. See yourself doing or being or having what you want. See it with faith and the determination to put forth every effort toward its achievement.

When you do this, when you have decided, "This is what I want!" you magnetize, instantly, the creative power within you. This power begins to charge the very "mental ether" about you; it reaches out through time and space toward the "iron filings"—the opportunities you need in the form of conditions, circumstances, resources and people—to attract all the "elements" required to help make what you have pictured come true.

Until you make a positive move in the direction of the things you desire, you will attract nothing worthwhile. Minus decision, you cannot properly magnetize the power within you. An unsettled state of mind attracts only unsettled conditions.

Keep the idea of the magnet and iron filings in mind as you face different problems in life. Ask yourself: "What am I attracting by my thoughts and desires? Only negative happenings?"

If your mind is filled with fears and worries and doubts, it is charging the atmosphere about you with uncertainty. You are making yourself susceptible to conditions and circumstances which can cause you to fail in your endeavors.

And here is an important point to remember: the deeper you desire to accomplish something, the stronger is your power of magnetization.

Let's suppose this power within is a servant, capable of following your every bidding, without question. Now, if you should order this servant, in a casual sort of way, to "bring me a glass of water," you would expect the servant to answer your request, but take his time doing it. However, if with a feeling of great urgency you should demand, "Quick—bring me a glass of water!" the chances are the servant would deliver it to you in a hurry.

This is exactly how your subconscious operates. It functions slowly or swiftly on commands which you give it by your conscious mind, dependent exactly on how deeply you really mean it!

You've heard people say, "I set my heart on this or that—and I got it!"

Certainly they got it! They couldn't help but get it. Their desire was so strong that it created a terrific power of magnetic attraction . . . and everything about them—things and people—was affected by it.

Start living in the consciousness of what you want. Clothe it with your desires; see it happening in your mind's eye; have faith it is going to happen; put forth every effort to help make it happen; keep the "mental ether" magnetically charged with the mental pictures of your objective.

Do this—and step by step you will draw to you what you need to cause the "iron filings" to group themselves in the form of opportunities about you and eventually materialize what you have wanted.

They used logic, planted tin cans and innocently waited for the harvest.

LOGIC AND THE UNKNOWN

by W. CLEMENT STONE

A small glass-bottomed boat approached the sandy beach of Rum Point on Grand Cayman Island in the British West Indies. Gleason, the native skipper, stopped at a coral reef . . . put on his skindiving helmet . . . checked his spear gun . . . dove into the water and swam among the coral rocks. Within six minutes he brought up five lobsters, three red snappers and three conch shells.

Conch salad properly seasoned . . . fresh, tender, juicy lobster boiled in salt water . . . snapper wrapped in aluminum foil and cooked over an open fire on the beach—what a lunch! And the conversation among the five of us was fascinating, informative and inspiring, too. For I'm a good listener—always searching for stories of true life experiences.

Dr. Curtis Bowman, a well-known Chicago surgeon, related his African experiences and those of his wife, Martha B. Bowman, author of the fascinating book *Ebony Madonna*. Here's part of the conversation:

"It was when we were in the East Belgian Congo

that a wife of a missionary asked her houseboy, who had been with the family six years, 'What are you doing with the empty tin cans you take away each evening?'

" 'Don't you know?' was the reply.

" 'No, but I would like to. Please tell me. Just why do people buy them?'

" 'They buy them to use the same as you do,' the boy replied after some hesitation and with apparent amazement.

" 'I don't really understand. Won't you please tell me exactly what is done with the tin cans or how they are used?' the wife asked. And she was amazed when she heard his answer. I know I was. You will be, too. And here's his answer:

" 'When we get our freedom, we'll be rich. We'll have everything the white man has. Now we plant the tin cans . . . we bury them deep. Some day we too will grow automobiles.' "

I commented: "He reasoned logically from what his experience had taught him. For throughout his young life, he had seen beautiful flowers, edible crops and great trees grow from the ground. It seemed reasonable to him and his customers that tin cans, properly planted, would grow automobiles. But his reasoning, like that of many of us, was based on the wrong premises. For he didn't consider the *unknown*."

Dr. Bowman then told us of some of his experiences in learning about Africa.

"You see, my brother-in-law was a missionary in Africa for many years. With his instruction and help, we traveled from one mission to another—fifty-one mission stations in all. We talked the language of the missionary. The natives trusted us. They wanted to help us. We were well received everywhere. Although taking pictures of native dances is taboo, we were given the privilege to do so."

"In *Ebony Madonna* your wife tells a fascinating story of a native with leprosy who returned to his own village when cured. The natives didn't believe leprosy was curable and reacted accordingly. What about leprosy? What about the cures?" I asked.

"Africa has millions suffering from leprosy." And then he told me the thrilling, exciting experiences of Dr. Carl Kline Becker of Oicha Hospital, Oicha Buna, Congo.

"An average of twelve hundred patients a day are treated by Dr. Becker and his staff besides the more than twenty-eight hundred in his leper colony. Ninety per cent of the patients are cured. Of course, if an arm is eaten away, a new one is not grown, but the disease is arrested and the patient is permanently cured."

As you have seen: The missionary's houseboy used logic, but the truth of how automobiles come into existence was *unknown to him* . . . he was ignorant of the facts. The cure of the dreaded disease leprosy is even today *unknown to millions*. Yet 90 per cent of the patients are cured in the leprosarium. One hundred per cent can be cured if given medical attention in time.

So in reasoning, let's *start with what we do know;* use logic; but before coming to conclusions, let's reckon with the *importance of the unknown.* For: *Truth will be truth regardless of any person's ignorance, disbelief or refusal to try to understand.*

Each day, man's increasing knowledge of cycles is guiding his forecasts and plans for the future.

CYCLES . . . AND YOU!

by EDWARD R. DEWEY

Cycles are the simplest thing in the world, at least in principle. Let me give you an example.

Suppose you are visiting my house and, looking out of the window, notice a bus pass by at 10:00 A.M. Half an hour later, at 10:30, you notice another bus pass. At 11:00, you see another one. "Ah ha!" you say. "Buses here run every 30 minutes." You have discovered a cycle all by yourself, without benefit of slide rule or gobbledegook. Cycles are just as simple as that (in principle).

Now what?

Well, first of all, you have a basis for predicting the probabilities of the future. If we go to lunch and come out of the dining room at 1:05, you will know that you probably missed the 1:00 bus and that, *if the cycle is continuing*, your next bus will pass in twenty-five minutes. So you chat for about twenty minutes and leave at 1:25 in order to stand in the wind and the rain the least amount of time.

Of course, the schedule may have changed or the bus have been delayed by an accident. You can't count for sure on a bus at 1:30. You are merely playing *probabilities*.

Where you have regularity, you have predictability

—at least to the extent that the regularity governs and is not present by chance.

Now let's do some more supposing.

You are overlooking a street near the center of a small town. Every ten minutes or so ten to fifteen people come along, more or less in a group. Another cycle! Again you can make a prediction (with qualifications). More than this, with this regular result appearing before you, you have a right to assume a cause—if the time intervals have been regular enough and have repeated enough times so that the behavior cannot reasonably be the result of chance.

You don't know the cause but there is no law against guessing. So you guess that there is a bus station around the corner and that every ten minutes a bus comes in and discharges its passengers. If you then find out that there *is* a bus station, and that a bus does come in every ten minutes, your guess is bolstered. It is bolstered still more if you find that the buses arrive just about the time your groups of people have been coming. But you still don't *know* that your people are coming from the buses. You would have to go out on the street and around the corner to find out for sure.

You continue to watch and count the people. You see other patterns. Every other ten-minute group of people is bigger. Perhaps there is a second bus with a twenty-minute schedule that reinforces the crowd from the first bus.

This is really the whole story about cycles.

You can predict that part of the traffic that comes in regularly recurring bunches. You can *not* predict by your ten- or twenty-minute cycles the crowd of people that will come along when the feature of the local movie house is over. Your predictions are only *partial*. But they are good as far as they go *if* the cycles keep on coming true, and *if* you have timed them right.

Moreover, by finding something else (in the example given, a bus schedule) with regularly recurring cycles of the same length, you get a clue as to possible cause and effect relationship. But to make sure, you need to run your clue down.

Almost everything fluctuates with rhythm, that is, in more or less regular cycles. Putting it another way, almost everything acts as if it were influenced by regularly alternating up and down forces which first speed it up and then slow it down.

Everybody would know this fact were it not for two things. First, in addition to the cycles there are accidental (random) fluctuations in things, too. These randoms hide the regularities so that at first glance you do not see them. Second, things act as if they were influenced simultaneously by several different rhythmic forces, the composite effect of which is not regular at all.

If we had several moons, the ups and downs of the tides would be very irregular. All the other moons would mix things up. It might have taken us much longer to find out about the tides.

If you have a long enough series of figures with which to work, it is not too hard to separate the different regular cycles from each other. When this has been done, you can project each regular cycle into the future and you can easily find out the combined or composite future effect of all the various cycles. When you have done this, you have a preview of what is going to happen: (a) *if the cycles continue,* and (b) *except as the cycles may be upset or distorted by accidental random noncyclic events.*

"Why wouldn't the cycles continue?" you may ask.

I'll give you one reason: The cycles may have been present in the figures you have been studying merely by *chance.* The ups and downs which come at more or less regular time intervals may have just happened to come that way. The regularity—the cycle —is there all right, but in such circumstances it has no significance.

How can you tell in any given instance whether or not the regularity you see is the result of chance or of a real underlying cyclic force?

The answer is, if the cycle has repeated *enough* times with *enough* regularity and with *enough* dominance, the chances are that it is the result of real cyclic forces.

Let me give you an example: Pick up a pack of playing cards and start to deal. The first card is red; the second is black; the third is red; the fourth is black. You have two waves of regular cycles—red, black; red, black. But this sequence could easily come about by chance. You continue to deal: red, black; red, black. Four times in a row now, this regular alternation. It could still be chance, but it couldn't be chance very often. Continue to deal. Red, black; red, black; red, black. Seven times now! It could still be chance, but it is less and less likely. It begins to look as if somebody had stacked the cards. You go through the entire deck. Twenty-six times! "Somebody certainly stacked the deck," you say. "It couldn't happen this way by chance once in a million times."

Exactly the same sort of reasoning applies to the cycles that you see in the ups and downs of the stock market, or the sales of your own company, or the weather, or anything else in which you may be interested. The more the cycle has dominated, the more regular it is, *and the more times it has repeated*, the more likely it is to be the result of a real cyclic force that will probably continue. If it has not dominated enough or has not been regular enough, you must have more repetitions to get equal assurance.

Well then, suppose that there are these rhythmic cycles in something. Suppose further that you have some knowledge of cycles, so what?

By using nothing more complicated than simple arithmetic (and a lot of work), you can find the cycles. By seeing how many times and how regularly each cycle has repeated in the past you can have a pretty fair idea of its significance (whether or not it is chance behavior). And by projecting all the significant cycles into the future, you can get some light on what is ahead *insofar as the cycles govern*.

In weather, we are used to forecasts in terms of probabilities. "The probability for the Chicago area is for snow." When you hear such a forecast on the radio, you don't rush out to put on your chains. The weatherman may be wrong. You wait for the snow to fall. *Then* you put on your chains. But the forecast warns you that snow is *likely* and, on the strength of this fact, you do make sure that you have your chains with you. If you are to make use of cycles in your business or your stock market forecasting, you are going to have to use the same approach.

Cycles are not the whole answer but, on the other hand, they are indispensable in attempting to arrive at the whole answer.

Cycles remind me of women. Women are not perfect (with individual exceptions, I hasten to add). But they are the best thing so far invented for their purpose. Until something better comes along, we will have to make shift with them as they are—or else miss the values they have to offer. Let's find out all we can about them!

Every day we encounter new ideas, and now here's . . .

A NEW WAY TO SAY THANKS

by CLEO GEHRKE DuBOIS

One of the most thankful persons in the world is Edward L. Kramer, president of Sterling Manufacturing, St. Louis, Missouri.

Kramer, back in 1948, wanted to convince his children—two sons and a daughter—that if they looked for the good life they'd find it. He had been telling them this for a long time; but felt that to really impress them with his philosophy, he should find a more graphic way of doing so.

He started by asking them to be on the lookout for good in three people each day. "This good can be in your playmates, in your neighbors, in your teachers —in anyone with whom you come in contact," he told them. Each night Kramer sat with his children and helped them write brief notes of appreciation to these persons. He made sure that the postcards were mailed.

At first it was hard for the children to do this, and there was the complaint, "I can't think of anybody to write to," but soon they began to discover much good in people that they hadn't perceived before.

Kramer was persistent and followed through faithfully in experimenting with his idea. Soon his youngsters began to notice that the happiness they gave to others by their thoughtfulness bounced back to them multiplied, not just from the persons to whom they had written but from many people and many sources.

The ordinary government postcards on which the family wrote their first thank-you notes were replaced with a specially designed yellow Thank-U-Gram, which looks like a telegram and which carries the same strong impression of importance and urgency.

The response from persons receiving Thank-U-Grams led Kramer to expand his idea. "Since they are doing so much to help our family, why not let others use them to bring themselves happiness?" he reasoned. From then on a two week's free supply of Thank-U-Grams went out with an answer to every inquiry concerning them.

There was, however, one stipulation which Kramer made. Each person receiving the gift had to agree to look for two points of good in people every day, had to promise to mail the two Thank-U-Grams without fail. To date, the "Thank-You Man" has given away nearly two million Thank-U-Grams to people who, like himself, want to look for the good in others and find it.

A salesman who earns a five-figure income annually working for Ford Motor Company says: "The day after delivery of a new car or used unit, I mail the customer a Thank-U-Gram. If I talk to a prospect, and he doesn't buy, I mail him a Thank-U-Gram next day. When a customer or a bird dog sends me a sales lead, I mail him a Thank-U-Gram."

This man, an insurance salesman before going to work for Ford, says, "The unusualness of the Thank-U-Gram is the best personal advertising I could do."

I read about the Thank-U-Grams in a religious weekly newspaper. It was years after that before I received one addressed to me. Kramer's foundation name and address were on the back, so I immediately sent for my trial supply.

Like the Kramer children, I, too, found it difficult

at first to think of two persons to whom I could show appreciation each day. But as my faculty of appreciation developed, I began to notice that the number of persons who benefited me in some way began to increase like magic! I found it frustrating to choose only two persons to admire and usually wrote more Thank-U-Grams when time allowed.

Kramer had instructed me: "Send them to anyone who has brought some good into your experience during the day—a cab driver, a client, a customer, a minister, a TV performer, an author, a friend or a stranger. You must promise me, though, to send a minimum of two Thank-U-Grams a day, even though you have to search hard for things to appreciate.

"Don't let a day go by without fulfilling your promise and I guarantee you that your life will become richer with your efforts."

Kramer, the "Thank-You Man," was right. Thank-U-Grams are definitely helping me to develop the rewarding habit of being more appreciative, a habit that can best be developed through deliberate practice. I can say without a doubt that looking for the good in others is a practice that returns one's investment a hundred fold!

When I commented to Kramer about my experiences with the Thank-U-Grams, he wrote back: "Others, too, have found that an awareness of good is not so much a special gift but an acquired faculty. In other words, it is achieved by directed attention."

Thank-U-Grams are purposely postcard size to help people realize how very little time it takes for one to show appreciation or praise. "No one can use the excuse that he doesn't have time," declares Kramer. Conciseness and brevity are the keynotes of the following Thank-U-Grams which Kramer himself has written and sent:

To a minister: "Your Sunday sermon was a gem. It stays with me and continues to inspire me."

To a TV star: "Your show Tuesday was the highlight of the day's broadcasting. You are most welcome in our living room."

To a cab driver: "It isn't too often that I enjoy a cab drive as I did yesterday. Your courtesy and consideration were deeply appreciated. You are a credit to your craft."

For a public utility: "I am so likely to take many good things for granted. I feel that I must thank you for the way you provide this most necessary service to our home."

To a clerk: "You were so patient in waiting on me today. Your kindness made it possible for me to get exactly what I wanted. Thank you!"

For a service: "Thank you for your prompt response to our call. You saved the day for us."

To a customer: "Thank you for the audience you gave me yesterday. It made it possible for me to show you how well we can serve you. Thank you again!"

To the mayor: "Your stand for the bill that will do so much for our city made me proud of you. You are serving your community well."

With Kramer's permission, I have adapted the Thank-U-Grams to meet my own needs. For example, I am fairly good about remembering to be aware of the blessings which come to me from outsiders, but I need desperately to cultivate more appreciation towards members of my own family. Therefore, I now write one Thank-U-Gram each day and mail it, but the other I write to some member of my own family. For example:

To Greg, our son: "Thanks so much for repairing the vacuum cleaner. It is a very important 'tool' to Mother and we just couldn't get along without it!"

Many world leaders and famous persons believe strongly in Kramer's idea of cultivating an awareness of good as a means for finding happiness and success. The following persons, Mr. Kramer told me, are among the many who have used and promoted his Thank-U-Grams: Dinah Shore, Harold Macmillan, Arthur Godfrey, Leonard Bernstein, Bob Hope, Loretta Young, Jack Benny, Lucille Ball, Henry Ford II, Walt Disney, Jack Paar, Arlene Francis, Robert Frost, Eddie Cantor, General Dwight D. Eisenhower, and Jerry Lewis.

Dr. Norman Vincent Peale is a regular user of Thank-U-Grams. He says, "I send them, often unsigned, to friends, strangers, anyone who has done something admirable."

To get a trial supply of Thank-U-Grams, write to the Kimball Foundation, Brentwood, St. Louis, Missouri. Just write, "I agree to use Thank-U-Grams according to Mr. Kramer's plan and send two every day." A ten-day supply will be sent you free as often as you write. You may include postage, but it is not required.

Because of his unusual project of promoting the art of thankfulness, Edward L. Kramer is called "the most thankful man in the world." He is probably doing as much as any other living person to help people look for the good in their lives and find it.

*Meet an employer who advocates reading
on the job and thinking with your feet—
on the desk.*

READ AND RELAX FOR PROFIT

by CLAIRE COX

What would your boss do if he found you tilted back
in your chair, feet upon your desk, reading a book
or magazine on company time?

Would he fire you?

Not if your boss was Norman L. Cahners, millionaire inventor, innovator and chairman of the board of
the Cahners Publishing Company—and if you were
reading something to help you in your work.

Cahners, a robust man with an easy smile, not only
has *no* objection to putting feet on desks and reading
at work; he encourages both. Early in his highly
successful publishing career, which was launched with
an invention that helped win World War II, Cahners,
now forty-five, realized that one of the secrets of being
a good employer was in practicing what you preach.
What is right for the boss, he concluded, is right for
his employees. Men and women like to work for a
person who encourages them to forge ahead.

This employer likes to sit back with his feet on his
desk. He also believes in reading at work, if the
material is pertinent. So enthusiastic is he about both,
in fact, that he has launched a campaign for on-the-job
reading programs throughout business and industry
to increase efficiency at work and relaxation at home.

Being an idea man, Cahners has made his own foot-on-desk reading periods as comfortable as he can. He did it by inventing a special footrest. When he wants to think, dictate or read, he pulls out the top drawer of his desk in his peaceful, uncluttered, seventh-floor Boston office, places a small footrest on it, leans back and swings his feet into position. He may look as if he is taking it easy, but he maintains that some of his most constructive work is done in this restful posture.

"Employers should encourage on-the-job reading," he says, "as long as it has something to do with the work. To keep abreast of developments, it is difficult to read at home, what with the competition from television and other distractions."

To illustrate how complicated the reading problem can be, Cahners has listed 2,160 technical and industrial publications in this country alone. There were 1,800 in 1949—and only 10 in 1850. The total circulation of all such publications last year was more than 43 million—with far more actual readers.

"The technical man never stops working," Cahners explains. "His leisure time and shorter working hours give him more time—more time for homework from work and it is increasing every day."

Cahners, by being what Madison Avenue calls "a thinking man," has solved his own problems on this score. He supervises the publication of fourteen industrial and trade magazines, serves as a corporation director, engages in a number of philanthropic activities and still finds time to putter around his suburban Brookline, Massachusetts, home with his wife and three children and engage in his favorite pastime—sailing off Bar Harbor, Maine.

Ever since he can remember, Cahners has been a man in a hurry. At Harvard, he set a record of 9.3 seconds for the 100-yard dash that no one has been able to beat. He was a member of a U.S. Olympic track team after he graduated from Harvard in 1936, and still is remembered at Harvard for his prowess on the football field.

Born to a well-established family, Cahners attended Phillips Academy at Andover, Massachusetts, graduating in 1932. He is a member of the Andover Alumni Council, where his pet interest is in setting up scholarships so poor but worthy boys can attend the famous Ivy League prep school.

Cahners always has worked for himself—except for his hitch in the Navy. His first job after college was selling furniture on the installment plan to rural New Englanders. Before long, he had several hundred persons stumping the countryside for him. He learned quite a bit about merchandising on that job—enough to win him a naval decoration later and start him on the road to bigger things.

The day after Pearl Harbor was attacked, Cahners decided not to wait for his draft board to call him. He left his job and enlisted in the Navy. Because of his experience in moving furniture from factory to home, he was assigned to try to help solve the huge wartime problem of getting supplies to the fighting men.

What did Cahners do? He went into action—Cahners style—by sitting back, putting his feet on a desk and pondering. The result was a series of highly technical but unusually workable innovations, including the use of a pallet contraption that became the standard wartime shipping platform for everything from ammunition to chocolate bars.

The Navy awarded Cahners a special citation. Then, at official request, he wrote a publication on war matériel handling. It was a Navy periodical, but requests for copies streamed in from civilian manufacturers.

This is what really set Cahners, the old track star, into high speed. After he left the service, he received official naval approval to convert his Navy publication to peacetime use. He changed "matériel" to "materials" in a new magazine called *Modern Materials Handling*, which he gave away to persons he thought should have it, letting the advertisers foot the bill. By using that magazine as a foundation, he has built a publishing empire.

In the course of expanding his activities, Cahners gave himself—and Western Union—a boost by using the telegraph company's facilities to make surveys of regular readers and seek new ones. This was so successful that Western Union now has an entire department devoted to making special canvasses for businesses.

Cahners hopes to bring his two sons into his business with him, but one of them is such a chip-off-the-old-rugged-individualist-block that he wants to branch out on his own. Both boys attend Andover, but Cahner's dream for both of them to be Harvard men will not be realized.

As the fourteenth member of his family to attend Harvard, Cahners naturally wanted to make it unanimous with Robert, who is seventeen, and Andrew, who is fifteen. But Robert has his own ideas. Being independent, he made his own college arrangements and will enter Dartmouth in the fall.

Robert wants to be a publisher, but of his own periodicals, not his father's.

Andrew has not made up his mind yet, but is following in his father's footsteps in at least one respect. He is already a track star at Andover though still only a freshman.

The third Cahners child is nine-year-old, red-haired

Nancy, described by her doting father as "the light of my life."

Mrs. Cahners, the former Helene Rabb, is a charming woman who shares her husband's love of people and working with them. She is president of the Beth Israel Hospital women's auxiliary in Boston.

This full-time, nonpaying job includes two secretaries and an office staff. At thirty-nine, Helene Cahners is the youngest president ever to serve the 8,300-member organization.

As is the case with many a wife, Mrs. Cahners had to bide her time for quite a while before getting her first mink coat. Her husband, who admits to being economical despite the fact that he is a millionaire, explains why. "I had to sit with my feet on my desk and think about it for a while first," he says.

History is full of individuals who became a success by . . .

THINKING BIG IN SMALL PLACES

by DR. HAROLD BLAKE WALKER

A recent magazine article suggested the possibility of decorating small homes and apartments with big ideas. The author noted that good decorating "expands space," makes small rooms look large and attractive, and provides an atmosphere congenial to personal growth. Essentially, the article suggested that we need to learn the art of "thinking big in small places."

When it comes to decorating I am a neophyte, but I am acutely aware that thinking big in small places is one clue to the mastery of life. Most of us start in small places, small jobs, little homes, obscure occupations, and what happens to us depends on the kind of thinking that goes on in us while we are seemingly buried in half-forgotten locations. If our thoughts are small and mean, we stay small and mean, but if our thinking expands our horizons and enriches our condition, we grow in grace and knowledge.

If ever a man needed to expand his living space it was Jesus. He was born in a stable in an obscure suburb of Jerusalem because "there was no room for him in the inn." He grew to maturity in a carpenter shop attached to his home in an unpretentious village called Nazareth. The place was so obscure and unimportant that Nathaniel was led to wonder "Can anything good come out of Nazareth?" Jesus never traveled beyond the borders of Palestine, a tiny country that could be fitted more than once into the state of Illinois.

Nevertheless, the world's most significant thinking was done in the town of Nazareth, and from it there emerged one who would be known as Lord and Master. What mattered most was not the town, not the quality of the schools, not the nature of the community, nor the vigor of the synagogue, but rather the person who found in the town, the school, the synagogue and the community something more than anyone else found there. Jesus captured from His environment all the values it offered and then enriched it with His own insight.

Nevertheless, who would have guessed that the faith and hope of Christendom would have come out of Nazareth? Who, for that matter, would have dreamed that the age of air travel would be born in Kitty Hawk, a place nobody ever heard of until the Wright brothers made it famous. Or who would have guessed that the character of Abraham Lincoln would have come out of a log cabin in Kentucky? You never can guess what great things can come from out-of-the-way places when somebody begins to think greatly. A recent editorial called attention to the late Professor Ahmed Bokhari, Pakistan diplomat and citizen of the world. He came, literally, from nowhere, but the editorial noted that "his spirit, like his mind, knew no narrow frontiers."

Too often we are inclined to feel it is a misfortune when our children, for one reason or another, can't go to one of the great colleges or universities and have to settle for a college of second-rate standing. It seems curious, though, that in *Who's Who* the little schools have more than their share of distinguished graduates. What is more, the famous schools have at least their share of the failures. The point of the matter is that where people come from isn't nearly as important as the spirit and purpose inside them. Speaking of the meager educational opportunity of Abraham Lincoln, Lord Charnwood wrote, "There is some advantage merely in being driven to make the most of a few books; great advantage in having one's choice restricted by circumstances to good books." Lincoln, like Jesus, thought big in small places.

*Nothing is impossible and here's a bottle
cork to prove it . . .*

IMPACT

by MARJORIE SPILLER NEAGLE

In a gun factory in the United States, an unusual
experiment was conducted. A bottle cork, weighing
less than four grams, was suspended by an almost
invisible silk thread alongside a heavy steel bar, itself
hung vertically from a beam by a slender metal chain.

The cork, set in motion, began to swing gently
against the steel bar. For a long time there was nothing
to be seen but its rhythmic, noiseless swaying back and
forth, back and forth, while the bar remained motionless.

More minutes went by . . . two . . . five . . . ten . . . a
half hour. Then suddenly under the relentless barrage,
and so nearly imperceptibly as to seem almost an
illusion, the steel bar was seen to tremble. A few
moments later it shuddered as if seized with a nervous
tremor, hung quiet again, then shuddered again.

There was no deviation in the motion of the cork.
Steadily, without haste, it continued its noiseless assault. And now the movements of the great steel bar
became less tremulous as it settled into the beginning
of an orderly pattern of motion, gradually picking up
the rhythm of the swinging cork.

In another half hour the cork, its work finished, had
been cut down and the heavy bar was swinging back
and forth as steadily and as rhythmically as a pen-
dulum.

"There is a moral here someplace," I thought, as I pondered a comparison between the steel bar and any prejudiced person or group. When I encounter such seemingly immovable objects, I feel that I can do nothing about them.

"How can I, singlehanded," I ask myself, "make even the slightest impact on such hide-bound opinions? I am only one person. I would waste my strength and time for nothing."

So I do nothing.

But if an almost weightless cork can, by its gentle persistent hammering, set a heavy bar of steel in motion, why cannot I, with nothing more than a friendly *good morning* day after day, induce that standoffish neighbor of mine to become a friend?

Why cannot my quiet yet constant reiteration of a truth finally make an impression on the most deeply rooted prejudice?

And in a broader sense, cannot I, by continually speaking against an evil or a lack in my community, eventually influence other people so that the minority of one will become a majority large enough to correct that evil or that lack?

If a little cork can do it—so can I!

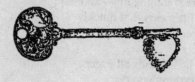

4 LOVE UNLIMITED

*To love is to place our happiness in
the happiness of another.*
      —Gottfried von Liebnitz

TO ANY LITTLE BOY'S FATHER

There are little eyes upon you
And they're watching night and day;
There are little ears that quickly
Take in everything you say.

There are little hands all eager
To do everything you do;
And a little boy who's dreaming
Of the day he'll be like you.

You're the little fellow's idol;
You're the wisest of the wise.
In his little mind, about you
No suspicions ever rise.

He believes in you devoutly,
Holds that all you say and do,
He will say and do in your way,
When he's grown up, just like you,

There's a wide-eyed little fellow
Who believes you're always right;
And his ears are always open
And he watches day and night.

You are setting an example
Every day in all you do;
For the little boy who's waiting
To grow up and be like you.

—Anonymous

*He discovered a symbol of true love when
he read ...*

THE LETTER ON YELLOW
SCRATCH PAPER

by W. CLEMENT STONE

The cab driver and I became quite friendly as we
conversed together while riding from Kennedy Airport
to uptown New York last Monday.

You see, I try always to make a cab trip in New
York pay off with a human interest story. And this
trip was no exception.

"Tell me about yourself and some of your experiences," I suggested. So Louis, the cab driver, told me
of a strange experience he had had the previous week.
And when he did, I felt he was ready—ready to talk
about himself and his family. So I directed his mind
in the desired channel with the question: "Are those
your four children?" referring to a picture on the
dashboard in front of the steering wheel. "Yes," he
answered, "they are wonderful kids. We have a lot of
fun together." And he kept talking.

By the time we were within a few blocks of my
destination, I sensed that he had an inner urge to
share with me something very personal to him. And
now I share it with you: a symbol of love—a letter
written on yellow scratch pad paper.

He had already shown me his wallet with a picture
of his wife when she was a bride and colored snapshots
of the children. He had a loving word to say about
each.

Now he handed me the letter. It was from his wife. She had handed it to him when she kissed him as he left the front door that morning.

"I suppose in every marriage there are arguments from time to time," he started. Then continued, "My wife and I had what some might call a family squabble last night. She was griping about our early marriage —when the children were younger, telling me how other husbands helped around the house and I did nothing.

"Said she, 'My brother Herman always helped Helen when the children were young. He would wash the dishes, even scrub the floors. And Irene's husband, Tom, would make necessary repairs to the furniture —he'd even change the baby's diapers and never complain. But you—you weren't helpful at all when the children were young. You weren't a good father then.'

"You see," he apologized to me, "as a cab driver I worked twelve hours a day. And my job was to make the money. I made good money because I made every hour count. Then when I got home, I was tired. I needed sleep and some relaxation.

"And look what we have to show for it," he continued. "A home of our own in Queens, a good Chevy car, life insurance, some money in the bank and a summer home in upstate New York. In the summer the family is on the lake. I spend Fridays, Saturdays and Sundays with them. Because they are away, I work an extra four hours Mondays, Tuesdays, Wednesdays and Thursdays."

I began to read the letter and as I did so I felt the emotions of its writer. Now you will feel it too because of the love and sincerity with which it was written. For the following is part of what I read:

"I was wrong in finding fault with you. I was dead wrong in complaining about what you didn't do when the children were younger. I am humiliated that I complained you weren't a good father then. For I know of no husband or father that is more loving, kind and thoughtful of his children and wife. You are certainly doing the right thing for all of us.

"And it was wrong for me to allow my feelings of the past to interfere with our happiness now. For we do have a happy home. And now it is I who, with faultfinding and nagging, have brought unhappiness to you.

"I love you so very much. I have the most wonderful husband in the world. And my children have a most loving and kind father. I hope you will forgive me."

And as I handed the yellow page back to Louis, he said, "This letter: It will never be forgotten. For I will keep it forever."

Christmas, from now on, will have a deeper meaning for you after you understand . . .

KELLEY'S CHRISTMAS GIFT

by OG MANDINO

The month of December was cold and wet and gloomy in England in 1944. Although the tides of war had shifted in favor of the Allies, our casualties still continued high so our morale matched the weather.

Our B-24 airbase, fifty miles north of London, was just like a hundred others spread carelessly over the face of England and we were similar to all the others in planes and personnel with one exception—we had Kelley.

I don't remember his first name but I do recall he was a navigator . . . and a good one. Kelley had habits that set him apart from most of us who assumed a phony air of boldness to hide our fear. For one thing he was older than most of us . . . probably near thirty. When we went to London every two weeks and raised unholy hell he remained behind and wrote letters to his wife, his mother, his son and every other relative whose address he kept in a little brown book. A forty-eight-hour pass to Kelley meant stuffing his duffel bag with candy bars and canned food and bringing it to poor families in the village. Before each mission Kelley attended chapel services while most of us slept those extra fifteen minutes. Yes, to many of us, Kelley was a strange guy.

Then, about two weeks before Christmas, Kelley got an idea. He decided that we would throw a Christmas party on our base for all the British kids that lived in the area. He sold the idea to our Colonel and then he assigned projects to all of us. It was difficult to say no to Kelley . . . and when we weren't flying missions we had plenty of time on our hands anyway.

Kelly set up collection boxes inside the Post Exchange and I painted signs that asked for contributions of candy bars, chewing gum, canned fruit and cookies from each man's weekly allotment purchase. We filled dozens of boxes.

Then Kelley coaxed the mechanics on the flight line to make toys from spare parts and scrap metal. The carpenters got into the act and began building toy carts and crude rocking horses and even the nurses made stuffed dolls and animals. Everyone became involved and Kelley kept the whole operation coordinated in a way that would have made General Motors proud.

Two days before Christmas, the mess hall began to look like Macy's warehouse . . . and Kelley was all smiles . . . until someone reminded him that we had no Christmas ornaments or lights to hang. He solved this problem as swiftly as he solved the others. He commandeered boxes of silver chaff that we dropped during our bombing missions to confuse the enemy radar . . . and we had our "icicles." He had the base electrician wire a couple of hundred spare wing-tip lights to heavy cable and we spent a morning coloring them with paint that he produced from Lord knows where.

On Christmas eve we decorated the mess hall and although it was no Rockefeller Plaza we were all proud of our handiwork . . . even though none of us would admit it. On the way back to our barracks we got the "good news." We were flying a mission on Christmas Day. You can imagine the remarks next morning before, during and after the briefing. We were all thinking the same thing . . . what a day to die! Our mission, of course, wasn't going to affect the Christmas party. The base personnel all had their instructions from Kelley and all the buses from the motor pool had been assigned a special town or hamlet where they were to go to pick up the children.

When we returned on Christmas afternoon, from what had been a rough mission, we hurriedly changed clothes and dashed to the mess hall as soon as de-briefing was finished. The place was bedlam. It looked like recess time at my old grammar school. Kids were pushing their new carts and toy trucks, little girls skipped and danced with their new stuffed dolls clutched tightly to their breasts, while the boys ran from one end of the hall to the other holding their miniature planes and imitating the sound of Spitfires and P-51's. Every smiling face was smeared with chocolate . . . many for the first time ever. The wingtip lights blinked overhead in multicolored joy and someone had found a phonograph which was playing tinny but recognizable Christmas carols. I watched for a few moments remembering many happy childhood Christmases of my own. Then I left and slowly walked back to my barracks. In the distance someone gunned all four motors of a B-24, drowning out the joyous shouts from the hall.

I passed the chapel and then I stopped. Without even knowing what I was doing I found myself walking back up the cobblestone walk and pulling open the metal door.

I stepped inside for the first time since I had been on the base. The outside world quieted down. I felt myself kneeling and before I could stop myself I was sobbing. It was the first time I had cried since my mother had died. Finally I prayed . . . prayed for Kelley and the rest of his crew whose plane I had watched explode into flames after taking a direct hit only a few hours ago.

Since that Christmas, so many years ago, I never hear a Christmas carol or watch a child open a Christmas gift without remembering Kelley and counting my own blessings. Why Kelley is not here to enjoy each Christmas like the rest of us is a question I stopped asking myself. . . . I finally realized that Kelley's gift to all of us was the same priceless gift of sacrifice and love that we all received from Him whose birthday we celebrate on Christmas Day.

Finally, there comes that wonderful moment when all your sacrifices as a parent are rewarded . . .

MY WHITE SHEEP

by NOVA TRIMBLE ASHLEY

It's almost nine o'clock on this sultry June morning in Pittsburgh, Pennsylvania, and I'm dripping with perspiration. If it had rained, the commencement exercises would have been held inside one of these impressive old buildings; but since it didn't rain, this graduating class of the Carnegie Institute of Technology will receive their degrees out here on this lovely, green-carpeted campus mall.

Now I'm fanning myself with the commencement program and my daughter-in-law Pat tells me I'm just nervous; she insists the humidity is no more uncomfortable here than at home in Wichita. Pat's parents and sister Carole and my husband have settled themselves on wooden, folding-type chairs; and my little granddaughter Traci is standing and peering over the crowd—watching for her Daddy.

People continue to stroll in. None of this seems real to me. . . . I can't believe that our son Kenneth is a member of a group of young scientists and engineers who will receive recognition here this morning. Looking back, however, it seems to me Ken was always sort of different. . . .

I remember the morning Ken was born. It was hot and sultry, like today. Depression days. A hot, dusty July. He was our second son, but this birth proved to be extremely difficult. The baby had become entangled in the umbilical cord; and when he was finally born, crushed and blue, he was beautiful only to me.

Poor little fellow, I had thought. Surely he must have been saved from death to serve some genuine purpose in life. I wondered if he would be a teacher, like his father—or maybe a minister! The baby had opened his unbruised eye—the other was too swollen to open—and he had looked at me with "O-my-God-Mother" disgust as if to say, "How dare you plan my life?"

At six months, Kenneth was adorable, fat, blond and serious, exploring outlets and cords on hands and knees, studying knots and wheels with earnest concentration. Big Brother, just two years old, constantly followed him with the protective arms of an archangel, only to be rewarded with sudden "conks" on his head.

It was a sorry day for us when Ken learned to use a screwdriver. Then everything with screws, from tricycles to high chairs, collapsed in his path. No playpen could hold him for long. When we hid the screwdriver, he sneaked a nailfile.

Ken ran into his first difficulty with the outside world when he started school. The teacher had said she didn't think Kenneth *liked* her very well. He rarely spoke and he wouldn't count.

"But anybody can see there's twelve things there," Ken had sobbed. "Six things and six more things, or seven things and five—and I don't wanta say 'one-two-three'—it's silly!"

Ken's father was the school principal. He warned his son, "Kenneth, you must learn to be obedient."

In second grade, art proved to be his downfall. Ken loved to draw and paint, but he rebelled when the teacher instructed the children to put features on the shadows they had drawn.

"Shadows don't have eyes and noses," Ken had stubbornly insisted. "I'm going to color my shadow black. Who ever heard of a shadow with eyes?"

It was never dull at our house! When Little Brother had an earache I searched in vain for our electric heating pad.

"Oh, Mama," said Little Brother, who approved of everything Ken did, "don't make Ken give it up! We're hatching little chickens for Easter, and this is only the seventh day."

"Kenneth Lynn Ashley," I screamed, "you get that heating pad this instant! And bring back my motor to the mixer, too, while you're in the garage."

"Mama," said Little Sister, "make Ken give me back the wheels to my skates! See—he's making scooters out of them for the boys! My good skates!"

"Mother, come quick!" Big Brother yells from the basement. "Ken's invention blew up and I think he's killed!"

But he wasn't dead, just frightened and singed. There was always a steady stream of inventions: telescopes from old eyeglasses and mailing tubes, wireless and wired communications of every imaginable conglomeration. We entered Ken's room at our own risk.

It was about that time that people began reminding us that Ken was blond and freckled, while his brothers and sister were brunet.

One evening after prayers, Ken whispered to me that he was the "white sheep" of the family. From that time on I referred to him as my "little white sheep" whenever we shared moments of closeness, which grew increasingly fewer as the years went by.

In junior high school there were paper routes (for he needed money for his research in the garage), track, basketball—all the things normal boys do, plus those ridiculous episodes: overhauling old automobiles and broken-down motor scooters; tearing the door off the garage when the homemade hoist didn't hold; helping to repair the motors of combines and trucks for wheat harvest; begging to get out of town during the summer months and follow the custom-harvest. He was too small, too young, but we let him go.

When he was thirteen he made a printing press. "So this is what you were doing all semester, instead of studying?" His father was discouraged.

Then Ken was in high school, and it was even worse. "Ken," I pleaded, "why aren't you studying for finals, too? Think of the grades you could be making—Kenneth, put that crazy, half-finished radio down and listen to me!"

And: "All right, you don't have to go to the prom, but you're going to your own commencement exercises if we have to drag you! Do you understand?"

High school completed, Ken joined the U.S. Navy. He was in communications, and he wrote: "Able, Baker, Charley. . . ." He was on a destroyer, the "Herbert J. Thomas."

"A destroyer?" Big Brother laughed. "Well, he's certainly had plenty of experience for it!"

Four long years. Finally Ken was home again. He decided to "give college a whirl" and to remain single all his life.

Ken enrolled in our municipal university that fall and in November he brought a pretty girl home.

"Mother, this is Patricia. . . . Dad, this is Patricia. . . . We're planning to be married next summer."

Just like that! Ken's father advised against it: "Ken, Patricia, don't you think you ought to wait until you've finished school? After all, with a family. . . ."

They laughed. "Oh, we're going to wait years before we have a family!"

They were married in July. Ken continued classes

and Pat got a job. A year and a half later their little girl was born.

"She's kind of small," Ken had said, "but real cute! It was mighty convenient of her to come during semester breaks, wasn't it? Very considerate of her."

They named her Patricia Lynn, for both of them; but we called her "Traci."

Things must have been pretty rough for them, but they worked hard. Traci was toddling pretty well by the time Ken received his B.S. degree, *cum laude,* from Wichita University. She looked cute trying to hold up the big tasseled cap while we snapped her picture.

Ken's major was electrical engineering, and offers of scholarships and fellowships poured in. He selected Carnegie Institute of Technology—and here we are today.

The processional is beginning now! The colorful kiltie band is playing, the pipes sound sweet and sad, and the skirt-clad musicians lead the way. Now the graduates, faculty members and other dignitaries are lining up across the way. Here they come! The wind is blowing now, and it isn't quite so hot. The long black gowns are fluttering in the breeze.

Traci points, "Here comes Daddy!"

I am gripping my camera! My husband whispers, "Please, I wouldn't take his picture now. Don't embarrass. . . ."

But I am running, running . . . here he comes! My son! Here comes my "little white sheep" now! His black robe blows about his thin legs; he takes long strides, and he has that dog-tired look of exhaustion on his thin face. But he is smiling a little, a half-serious thin little smile.

Now he is quite close to me and just ready to turn toward the crowd and march to his honored place.

I thrust my camera almost into his face. He sees me and his blue eyes grow horror-struck for an instant with that "O-my-God-Mother" expression. But then he smiles, as if in surrender to such idiotic maneuvers.

Then he is gone from our view. But I can no longer see anyway for the tears. Pat and I grab one another and sob quietly together. Such happiness! Such pride!

Composed again, we return to our places and the program is on its way.

In just a little while now, my son will be presented as a candidate for the doctor's degree in the College of Science and Engineering. A professor will announce his name, "Kenneth L. Ashley, Doctor of Philosophy," and place the heavy black cloth collar, lined with bright-colored, Scottish plaid, about Ken's shoulders. The audience will applaud.

Knowing my son, I am sure he will take the collar off in this heat just as soon as possible. But to me it is a sacred symbol that will be a part of him forever.

I shall never forget this moment, but I won't cry this time. Instead, I'll whisper his name to myself, *"Dr.* Kenneth Ashley," and I'll say a little prayer of thankfulness. My "little white sheep," may you serve humanity well!

*She was a stranger and he nearly rejected
her request ...*

AND THEN THERE WAS LIGHT

by EARLE STOWELL

Just a favor—granted almost grudgingly—changed my
whole life. And because of that favor, in thousands
of homes special lamps are lighted every night in
unknowing tribute to a man whose name I do not
know and to a woman's love for that man.

These lamps bring a warm glow to ranch houses
at the very end of the electrical lines in Arizona. They
press against the probing cold in rude farm houses in
Idaho. They light tiny homes of coal or copper miners
in Utah. They sit on tables in the homes of the humble,
the well-to-do and the wealthy across America. They
are treasured because each is handmade by someone
in the family or by a friend. The sparkling beauty of
the lamp is a constant reminder of that person's
achievement.

Few know the story of the lamp.

Shortly after the Second World War, I was quietly
going broke in a plastic-novelty manufacturing business. I had reached a state of numbness, where all I
could do was work, snatch a few hours' sleep and work
again—doing work I could no longer afford to pay
others to do.

This particular afternoon, annoyance swept over
me when a woman, in her mid-thirties and very pale,
entered the plant and put a cardboard box on the
counter. Her eyes focused somewhere above my head.

Words came in spurts like handfuls of confetti thrown at me. She wanted me to complete a pair of lamps for her.

Almost rudely, I said that I was running a factory, that I never did fix-it work. She didn't hear, for her words kept flicking out at me. I began to realize that her words had been rehearsed so many times that once started they had to keep tumbling over each other until they all came out.

She was trembling. I began to listen.

"I . . . I could pay . . . 50 cents each week. He left nothing . . . except these lamps . . . and . . . he couldn't even finish them for me."

Her fingers were white where she gripped the edge of the counter. A great shuddering sigh took complete possession of her. She fought for breath and went on. "He . . . did want to finish them . . . before . . . before. . . ." She stopped for a moment. "Friends are getting me a job. It won't pay much. But I'll be able to pay 50 cents a week. I . . . I don't care for how long. Charge anything." Tears began to flow down her cheeks.

Suddenly I was very small, very humble.

I looked in the box. The pattern of the lamps was evident, just plastic blocks to be piled up until the stack was high enough. A larger piece was to act as the base, smaller pieces for feet. My own voice wasn't under perfect control. I kept my eyes on the box.

"There's plenty of plastic here—some extra. At least enough to pay for the work." I forced my eyes to meet hers.

For a moment she swayed; the effort had drained her. She steadied herself and uttered a single word.

"When?"

"Wednesday."

She wheeled around. As the door shut behind her, "Thank you—may God bless. . . ." floated back.

I avoided working on the lamps. What did I know about making lamps? Besides, wouldn't I just be making something that would only remind her of her pain? I couldn't afford the time. Time was money; I had little of either.

It was Tuesday afternoon before I dumped the blocks out on the workbench. I hated that pile of plastic. I picked up one piece and began to grind and polish it. Suddenly I was riding the feeling of anticipation. The rough-cut blocks began turning into diamond-like pieces of polished crystal. I slowed down for the first time in months, took my time, enjoyed watching each block become perfect under my fingers.

Then I drilled a hole through each block and threaded them on a pipe nipple that was to hold them together and carry the electric wires. I added the base and the feet and set the lamp on the bench. Then I knew why I had dreaded the job. The lamp that should mean so much to the widow looked just like what it was—a pile of plastic blocks. I felt a little sick.

Then, almost as if someone asked, I wondered, "Suppose I turned every other block a quarter-turn?" Almost automatically I loosened the nuts on the nipple and shifted the blocks. It was magic. That pile of blocks was transformed into a beautiful crystal lamp fit to go into any home. With a feeling that approached reverence, I assembled the second lamp and placed it beside the first. A glow seemed to surround them.

On Wednesday, I found myself anticipating the woman's return. It seemed a long time before she walked timidly toward the door. She hesitated for a moment in the shade of the giant tree that blocked the sky from the window.

As she entered, I picked up one lamp in each hand

and set them before her. My eyes were fixed on hers. I wanted her to like those lamps—to really like them. But I wasn't prepared for the look of amazement that captured her face.

My eyes followed hers and I caught my breath.

A single piercing ray of bright sunlight had fought its way through the big tree outside the window. With pinpoint accuracy it struck the top of the nearest lamp. From there the light dripped from block to block, twisting, turning, reflecting as it went, making each polished surface burn with a pure white fire. The corners of the blocks acted as prisms, shattered the light and cast rainbows on the ceiling and down the walls.

As the tree branch moved back and forth, the ray of light struggled for freedom, only to be trapped in the lamp again and again. The whole room held something unreal.

She raised questioning eyes to mine. I nodded. A sudden sob shook her whole body. She gathered the lamps to her breast. "Thank . . . thank. . . ." she choked and stumbled out of the doorway. She made her way unsteadily to a car where someone waited for her.

A few weeks later the day came when the long months of overwork demanded their due from me. Four doctors, one after another, looked wise, shook their heads and said, "Subarachnoid hemorrhage. If you recover, you must never work more than four hours a day."

When I got out of the Veterans' Hospital, my business was gone. The dollars I had left wouldn't even buy a good lawn mower. Tangible assets were a few hundred dollars' worth of plastics, a small stock of cements and dyes. I had not been in the area long enough to establish roots that could nurture me at such a time. How could I support my family?

Then I thought of high-school students and their crafts classes. At a nearby high school, I asked for and received permission to demonstrate the working of plastic. I explained how to cut, shape and polish it. A student spoke up.

"That looks like fun, but what could we make of it?"

Hopefully I looked at the instructor. He shrugged.

"What can we make of it?"

I wasn't prepared for the question. Then, I sensed —rather than saw—the glowing lamps. I sketched a lamp on the blackboard. The instructor liked it. He bought half my plastic. A few more calls and my stock was gone.

Do you ever wonder if the big companies in America have a heart?

Back home, I wrote four letters. I pulled no punches. I simply stated my condition: questionable physical condition, no money, no assured market, only an idea. I sent one to a plastic manufacturer (probably one of the largest American companies), one to a manufacturer of metal lamp parts, one to a cement and dye manufacturer, and one to a lamp socket company.

The first three answered at once. They offered 90-day credit on more supplies than I needed. I bought lamp sockets at the dime store as I needed them.

Then a difficulty: Plastic was too expensive for schools to keep much on hand. I remembered how the first lamps had come to my shop in rough cut form. I cut parts for a hundred lamps and wrapped them with the necessary lamp fittings in separate packages. I offered these kits to the schools.

That started it. I was soon busy cutting and delivering lamp kits.

Yes, thousands of students and adults will light these lamps tonight. Thousands of lamps will burn in tribute to a woman's love—and to a man who wanted to finish a pair of lamps so that the woman he loved would not have to move in darkness.

---

*Love often reflects itself in a promise made
—and a promise kept . . .*

"AND THEY LIVED HAPPILY
EVER AFTER"

by W. CLEMENT STONE

"Daddy, you promised to read me a story."

That's what Lou Fink heard his four-year-old son Kent say. It was late Friday evening. Lou had arrived home from the office too late to have dinner with Kent. And Lou hadn't bothered to call Peg. Peg, like thousands of housewives and mothers, had worried while she waited as the minutes, and then the hours, passed by.

"The streets are slippery. He may have had an auto accident. Certainly Lou could have called," Peg thought. Peg didn't like the uncertainty, and she didn't like worrying.

But now that Lou was home, he could listen to Kent's prayers and then put him to bed. She could salvage the roast from the oven. So Peg went to the kitchen while Lou carried Kent to his bedroom.

"Daddy, will you tell me a story?"

"Daddy will tell you a story tomorrow night," Peg called out.

"Daddy, last night you promised me that if I went to sleep right away you would tell me a story tonight. And I did go to sleep right away. You promised me, Dad. You promised me."

Lou looked at Kent and said, "A promise is a promise, and a deal is a deal. Always remember that, son."

So Lou began to tell Kent the fairy tale of the six-year-old boy who was a friend to all the animals in the forest. He knew each of them by name, and he could speak their language. For he understood them and they understood him. And all this was possible because the boy had magical powers. But he had these powers only so long as he lived up to his promises.

Now, before Lou arrived at that part of the fairy tale where the young boy broke a promise to himself and consequently lost his magical powers, Kent fell asleep. He was tired. And perhaps the story had had a sleepy effect on Lou as well, for Lou himself was asleep when Peg awakened him and said: "Dear, dinner is ready. It may be burnt, but it's late and I'm half starved. I didn't stop for lunch today."

A promise is a promise and a deal is a deal kept flashing through Lou's mind as he and Peg chatted during their dinner. And that is quite understandable. For a great fairy tale has deep roots that reach into the subconscious mind.

After dinner Lou pushed his chair away from the table slightly, lit a cigar and said: "Did you know that a deal is a deal—a promise a promise?"

Peg only smiled. For she knew from experience that Lou was thinking out loud. She knew he would continue. And Lou did continue. "Decent people try to live up to their promises to other persons. Isn't that true? A person does try to live up to his promises to others."

Peg smiled and said nothing.

"But what about the promises to themselves? And what about all the New Year's resolutions that were made only a couple of months ago? Just think what wonderful things would have been achieved by people who made promises to themselves if they had lived up to those promises as diligently as they live up to their promises to others.

"And yet aren't promises to one's self just as important? Aren't they even more important than promises made to others? Shouldn't one try to live up to them just as diligently?

"And I have been thinking: Isn't it true that the difference between a successful person and mediocrity or failure is in proportion to that person's efforts to live up to the promises he makes to himself?

"I doubt if Helen would have had that heart attack had she lived up to her previous New Year's resolution to diet intelligently. We know she went to the doctor and he gave her a scientific diet. But after a few months she seemed to eat more than ever before.

"And Joe's family wouldn't be on relief. Joe wouldn't be sleeping in the gutters—if he had lived up to his New Year's resolution to stop drinking entirely.

"And how about Howard Smith? Howard wouldn't have been kicked out of Princeton if he had done his homework every day, just as he promised himself that he would last New Year's Eve at our party here."

Peg smiled.

"And, Peg, I made a promise too. And I just discovered what's really important to me is that I keep that promise to myself."

Peg stopped smiling, for she saw that Lou was

serious. Very serious. And she listened intently as he continued: "Peg, last New Year's Eve I made a solemn vow to myself. And I promised God that every day of the new year I would try to show my appreciation for the blessings He has given me: *you and Kent.*

"I promised to make you happy in those little things in which I have been lax."

Lou looked directly into Peg's eyes as he said, "Peg, you can count on me to be home in time for dinner in the future. And you know I do keep my promises to others. From now on I shall also live up to the promises I make to myself. Should an emergency arise, I shall at least telephone you in plenty of time. You won't need to worry. And I know the reason you do worry is because you love me so."

Peg smiled again. But she stopped listening. She came over and put her arms around Lou and kissed him. And then she confided: "I made a New Year's promise to myself too, I promised that the next time you came home late without notifying me, I wouldn't make your life miserable as I have in the past. It was difficult, but tonight I did live up to my promise. And, Lou, I did find that it pays to keep one's promises to one's self."

"And they lived happily ever after."

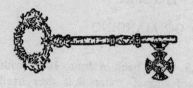

5 COURAGE
UNLIMITED

Courage grows from the heart.
                    —John Dryden

*He came back from the shadows of death
and inspired millions with hope.*

HOGAN

by OG MANDINO

They played the U.S. Open back in June, 1965, without the greatest professional golfer that ever lived. Ben Hogan, when told that he and all previous Open winners except the last five had to qualify for the "opportunity" to play in this year's Open, decided to sit this one out and watch television make heroes out of golfers that included many who never saw the day they could carry his golf clubs.

At the Colonial Open, a few months ago, Ben Hogan was presented with a trophy inscribed to "The Greatest Professional Golfer in History." As Ben accepted this award I wonder if the memory of a morning sixteen years ago flashed briefly across his mind.

Ben had just lost a play-off to Jimmy Demaret at Phoenix after winning the Bing Crosby Invitational and the Long Beach Open. He was tired and his thirty-seven-year-old legs were weary from the constant high pressure of tournament competition. He and his wife Valerie decided to pass up the next tournament at Tucson, and they headed for Fort Worth and home.

It was an early February morning in 1949. Patches of dark fog rolled like tumbleweed across prairie Highway 80. Ben's automobile headlights cut an abbreviated path through the mist. He drove slowly along the right shoulder of the road as he and Valerie, relaxing for the first time in months, chatted and planned their vacation. When Ben saw the oncoming headlights of a giant six-wheeler truck he inched closer to the culvert on his right. Suddenly two more head-lights appeared in the fog. They lined up with the first pair to fill the narrow road as a Greyhound bus at-tempted to pass the six-wheeler. There was no room for the Hogan car.

Ben instinctively threw his body across Valerie a fraction of a second before the car and bus collided with a sickening crunch. The impact slammed the car engine back into the passenger compartment and the steering wheel was driven through the driver's seat. Ben's effort to save Valerie had prevented his own instant death.

When his broken body was removed from the wreck-age it lay at the side of the road for nearly two hours because no one remembered to call an ambulance. Valerie, saved from serious injury by her husband's heroic action, watched helplessly as the little cham-pion's color continued to fade. After the ambulance finally arrived there was a tortuous drive of 120 miles to the Hotel Dieu Hospital in El Paso. Ben had a frac-tured pelvis, a fractured shoulder, fractured ribs and a shattered ankle. Worst of all he was suffering from severe shock.

For thirty days Ben lay immobile, his body encased in plaster from chest to toes. Then he met a tougher competitor for his life. A blood clot formed in his leg and began its journey toward his heart. Ben's desperate friends placed the dying man on an Air Force bomber and flew him to New Orleans. He was nearly dead when the famed surgeon, Dr. Ochsner, operated and tied off the vena cava, a large vein which funnels blood into the right auricle of the heart. Sports editors throughout the country began passing out assignments to prepare Ben Hogan's obituary while they awaited word from the hospital. They waited in vain.

A week after the operation, letters began arriving for Ben from every corner of the world . . . each with the same message. The sender was praying for Ben's recovery. As Ben said later, "I had never experienced anything like that and I guess it was because I never played up to the crowds. I had always concentrated so hard on making every shot that I never allowed myself to pay attention to the gallery. Now they were writing by the thousands and it was a humbling experience to know that so many strangers really cared what happened to me."

Within a month Ben was home and beginning the slow process of learning how to walk again. He weighed 96 pounds. That he would never play golf again was a foregone conclusion—except to Ben.

One morning, with sheer will power, he took his first step. He stumbled. He tried again and soon he was walking back and forth across the bedroom. Then he moved into the living room and began to complete lap after lap around the furniture while Valerie watched with pride and tearful admiration. Soon he began squeezing rubber balls to rebuild his arms and wrists.

One day he asked Valerie to bring him a golf club and using it as a cane he announced that he was going to walk around the block. The walks often seemed endless to Valerie, but Ben had developed his own system. He would walk as far as he could and then stop to rest. Each day he went farther and farther until finally he could circle the block nonstop. He was using the same system that had made him a champion: practice, concentration, practice, concentration. Because of his rearranged blood system his muscles continued to cramp and tire on him but he refused to quit. He tried swinging a club but the fractured shoulder and pelvis were taking long months to heal and his swing looked like that of a first-time-out duffer.

One morning in early fall an excited murmur raced through the Colonial Country Club. Members and club employees alike all stopped what they were doing and watched with fascination. Ben Hogan was on the putting green! Soon he began to walk with friends for a hole or two. In December he went out on the course and began playing . . . first one hole, then two, but the circulation still refused to function properly and his legs continued to swell. He carried a portable chair along and rested between shots. One day he tried playing an entire round. He paid for that by spending the next two days in bed.

In January, 1950, less than a year after his accident, Ben confounded every sportswriter in the country by entering the Los Angeles Open. Those in the know were betting that his legs would never carry him through the torturous 72 holes.

When he teed off for the first round, he had played less than eighty holes of golf since his accident. He came in with a 73! Next day he shot a 69! He followed that with another 69, and the same sportswriters who had written Ben off now began filling columns about the "comeback of the century." On the final day he tacked another 69 to his score, but Sammy Snead turned in one of the most sensational final rounds in the history of tournament golf and tied Ben with a 280 total for the 72 holes.

The following day Sam beat an exhausted Hogan in the play-off, but Ben was not disappointed. He had proven to himself that he was still a pro. He had also become a symbol for people with handicaps throughout the world, and another deluge of letters arrived at the Hogan residence. Now he was convinced that there was only one way to truly give these people the boost in morale they all sought. He had to win a major tournament. He set his sights on the U.S. Open in June.

The weather was hot and humid when the Open got under way at the Merion Country Club in Ardmore, Pennsylvania, on June 8. Sammy Snead was the favorite but the largest gallery followed Hogan. He shot a 72 on opening day which placed him eight strokes behind a young pro from Alabama who fired off a 64.

On Friday, Ben's putts began to drop and he limped in with a 69 to move within two strokes of the leader, Dutch Harrison. But Ben was already beginning to pay a horrible price in bodily torture. On the way back to the hotel with Valerie and his attorney, he had the car stopped while he fought off nausea and dizziness. Back in their hotel room Valerie helped him unwrap yards of rubber bandages from his swollen legs and then gently half-carried him to a warm bath where Ben sat for hours to ease the tightened muscles.

On Saturday he faced the toughest playing day of his career. Every nerve in his body seemed to be on fire while his legs, still swollen, had to carry him eight miles over 36 holes of pressure golf, 18 in the morning and another 18 in the afternoon. The temperature was in the mid-nineties and Ben was already drawing on that special reservoir that all champions have—guts.

He played the morning round in 72 and, since he always played against the course, not the individual players, he figured that another 72 in the afternoon would give him the championship.

When he teed off for the final round, the huge gallery could see the obvious pain in the little man's face but it never showed in his swing. Perfected by thousands of hours of practice and hardened by ten years of professional competition, the precision that prompted one writer to compare Ben's swing to "a machine stamping out bottle caps" was still evident.

Ben made one concession to his disabilities. He had his caddy pick the ball out of the cup after he holed out on each hole to save him from bending his knees. He clicked off the first nine in the afternoon in 36 but, after he teed off on the tenth hole, a knifelike spasm shot through his left leg. Momentarily he was unable to walk and by the time he had completed the thirteenth hole he had decided to quit. The pain was unbearable. He could not move his leg. But as he tottered off the green toward an official he remembered all the letters he had received. How many people would he disappoint? How many would quit in their own personal struggle to overcome a handicap if their idol, Ben Hogan, quit?

He stumbled toward the fourteenth tee. His body was drenched in perspiration, some from the weather, more from the pain.

He lost a stroke to par on the fifteenth hole and another on the seventeenth. Just before teeing off on the last hole an official told him that he needed a par four to tie for the championship. A pained smile flickered across Ben's face. If he parred this hole he'd have to come out here tomorrow and play eighteen more holes of torture against two of the best golfers in the business, Lloyd Mangrum and George Fazio.

His drive cut the heart of the fairway and, as he approached his second shot, he could already hear the standing ovation from the crowd surrounding the eighteenth green. Now his left leg was almost numb and there was a dull pain around his pelvic area. Common sense kept telling him to miss a shot and end the nightmare. He couldn't conceive playing another eighteen holes tomorrow; still his second shot was perfectly placed on the green and he was down in two putts to tie for the championship. The habit of always trying to do his best, no matter what the odds, had been too strong.

That night Ben slept the sleep of exhaustion but he arose refreshed and the swelling in his legs had almost disappeared. He played that day like the Hogan of old, shot a 69, and won the Open title by four strokes.

Ben won many more titles after that, but the indomitable courage of the little champion has placed those five rounds of golf high on the list of all-time athletic achievements. It was a triumph of mind and heart over physical adversity. It was an inspiration to millions who, day by day, struggle to overcome their own physical infirmities. It's a story that needed retelling because a new generation has already reached adulthood since Ben Hogan had his personal rendezvous with destiny on Highway 80.

But they wouldn't let Ben play in the Open. They thought he should "qualify." In my book he qualified a long time ago.

Arthritis couldn't strike out ex-pitcher Jerry Walsh.

STILL PITCHING

by ELEANORE PAGE HAMILTON

Eighteen-year-old Jerry Walsh took a deep breath, appraising the man at bat with narrowed dark eyes before winding up for the pitch. He flexed his arms and legs in practiced limbering of muscles, curved his fingers lovingly around the ball, and put his body into action with slow deliberation. Then something went wrong!

Agonizing pain gripped him. For a moment he was frozen with surprise, then he collapsed on the field. Doctors diagnosed his condition later as rheumatoid arthritis, thus putting a tragic end to a career recently opened to him by a tryout as a pitcher for the Boston Red Sox. The great crippler had struck again with characteristic suddenness and finality. For then, as now, no cure was known.

The trip back to his home town of Columbus, Ohio, was a nightmare of pain—physical and mental—for Jerry Walsh. He had been hailed as an all-around athlete both at St. Aquinas High School and later at Providence College. Now it was all over before he had had a chance to achieve his dream of being a major-league player. The vague stiffness in his legs, barely noticed at the times it occurred during his freshman year, was sentencing him to bed—"Too soon, dear God, too soon!"

Time had stretched monotonously into two years when Jerry became aware that Christmas, 1943, was on its way. He began to think about other Christmases and the many ways his widowed mother had devised to make them happy ones. She should have something pretty special this year for the demands he had been making on her storehouse of love and encouragement. But how could he, a bedridden cripple, earn money for a suitable gift?

Somewhere, he had read about careers in selling greeting cards. The more he thought about it, the more convinced he became that he could start such a business over his bedside telephone.

The result was "Jerry Walsh Greetings," which were sold through switchboard operators to employees in defense plants. His mother was delighted with her gift, of course; but more important, she saw the magic therapy of *interest in life* rekindled in her son.

The next step for Jerry was a shop in the hotel where he lived, staffed by handicapped people more mobile than he. He added novelties and executive gifts to his line, eventually expanding to branches in two shopping centers and a total of fifteen employees.

In 1944, when Jerry was just twenty-one, he and four bedfast friends founded Courage, Incorporated. This is still a going group with a board of directors— all handicapped—dedicated to building confidence and cooperation among kindred human beings. In their first ten years of operation, five hundred handicapped people were placed in jobs. "Our motto is a good one for combatting *any* discouragement," Jerry says. *"Do the best you can with what you have wherever you are."*

Three years later, Jerry Walsh took time off to enter the Mayo Clinic at Rochester, Minnesota. He underwent two successful operations that now enable him to get about with a crutch and a cane. "If you think I had troubles before," Jerry grins, "you should have seen me just trying to get out of bed after seven and a half years. The goal looked farther away than the Big Leagues ever did."

Not only did Jerry make it out of bed, but he has been a man on the go ever since. His efforts on behalf of the afflicted have been tireless. "Many arthritics can reach the point where they are able to perform jobs—and perform them well—with professional help and some personal willpower," he says.

Now a special educational consultant for The Arthritis and Rheumatism Foundation, Jerry has some one hundred and forty thousand miles of travel behind him in a crusade to alert the nation to the dangers of quackery. "The most shocking swindle in the country today," he declares, "is the $50 million taken from sufferers each year for fake 'cures.' "

Jerry has appeared twice before the Senate Special Committee on Aging to recount his personal experiences with such useless nostrums as sea water, alfalfa seeds, vibrators, and "souped-up" aspirin that has less pain-killing properties than the original drug. His testimony paved the way for legislation to prevent false advertising of products and devices that have been used to bilk some six million pain-stricken people annually.

In 1964, Jerry Walsh was presented with a plaque by President Johnson honoring him as the "Handicapped American of the Year." No one was more pleased than his wife Mary who, together with their two adopted children, had always known that Jerry was "the greatest."

Jerry is quick to point out that his return to normal living would have been postponed indefinitely if he had shunned medical aid for the more alluring will-o'-the-wisp offered by the exploiters. Treatment involves a complicated program; but the patient who works patiently with a skilled physician can look forward to eventually bringing his illness under control. "Arthritis can't be cured yet," Jerry emphasized, "but with courage and care, it can be conquered."

He left his legs in a foxhole but he still considers himself . . .

THE LUCKIEST MAN ALIVE

by RAYMOND A. TETZLAFF

Cheers of encouragement echoed through the halls of Percy Jones Hospital as war amputee Paul Kephart took his first cautious steps on his new artificial legs. He grinned right along with his appreciative audience of nurses, doctors and ward buddies as they watched him solo awkwardly on the limbs that would soon carry him back to a life of activity—and home.

"It was September, 1944, in Brest, France, when I lost my legs," Kephart reminisces. "The German shells were coming fast, shrieking and whining all around me. I plunged into a foxhole, but my legs stuck out. The next shell got them—quick and simple as that."

Paul literally got back on his feet at the hospital. He tells of endless hours of practicing: climbing stairs, walking in crowds, in and out of cars, up and down all manner of inclines. "I had to learn to walk all over again," he said. "But during the many months of uncertainty, anxiety and operations, those wonderful people at the hospital never let me give in to discouragement. Slowly, I began to realize that I had been given just one life to live, and that the way I was meant to do it was *standing up*."

Kephart now lives in a ranch-style house in Beloit, Wisconsin, with his wife and two pretty young daughters who like nothing better than to join their Dad in a variety of sports. "He's a good dancer, too," they add whenever they speak of his many accomplishments.

As a salesman for National Biscuit Company, he drives a car and walks, climbs and carries with the best of them. A recent incident reveals just how much of a workout he gives his stand-in legs. "I returned them to a manufacturer not long ago," he said, "because the rivets and bolts had pulled loose. They wanted to know why my legs showed such unusual wear. It gave me a good feeling to be able to confess that they got beaten up from bowling, golfing, kicking a football, playing basketball and even climbing up a ladder to fix my roof. Could be, I'm a little too rough on them."

Paul is president of the Elks Club bowling league. His average is 160, but he keeps aiming for the record he set for himself when he rolled a high of 256.

Doctors often ask Kephart to visit other amputees. It gives them encouragement to know a man who makes a good life for himself and his family, even though both legs are gone. "I usually try to leave such people with the thought that ruling out self-pity is the first step to rehabilitation," he says thoughtfully, doubtless recalling his own long struggle.

In 1947, Paul had an opportunity to prove that the roots of courage grow deep and strong within those who have found compensation for their handicaps. He was one of a party on a moonlight boat ride when another boat came hurtling out of the shadows to split his craft in two. Eleven people were thrown into the water. Kephart clung to the airhorns of the floating prow and managed to pull two struggling women to the safety of his bit of wreckage. Then, with one arm supporting them, he used the other to gather a frightened eight-year-old girl into his group to await rescue.

Kephart's remarkable ability to function bravely and effectively under such tragic circumstances caused Congresswoman Edith N. Rogers to report his feat to the government. It was made a part of the Congressional Record.

Paul Kephart's grin widens as he flips a deprecatory hand over all this. "Don't call me hero," he protests. "I'm just the luckiest man alive. I have everything— my family, home and friends. And best of all, I know that I can help others learn how to live. Sometimes I wonder just how grateful I can get!"

Paralyzed in a car crash, a promising young artist gained faith and fulfilled his destiny.

PORTRAIT OF COURAGE

by THEODORE VRETTOS

On a warm August day in 1951, a car carrying five boys sped wildly over a winding road on the outskirts of Exeter, New Hampshire. It was several minutes past one o'clock and the boys were anxious to return to their summer jobs in an apple orchard nearby.

Glen Fowler sat apprehensively in the rear seat while the car careened noisily around the sharp corners. Suddenly and without warning, the car came to a hairpin curve which the driver was unable to negotiate. . . .

In a matter of moments an ambulance hurried to the scene—four of the boys were rushed to Exeter's hospital. The fifth, Glen Fowler, was left in the wrecked car, presumably dead.

For two hours, Glen remained there unconscious. Then the ambulance finally came back for him, the doctors felt his pulse and discovered a faint beat. Quickly, they rushed Glen to the same hospital. But when the team of surgeons waiting there to operate on the boy saw him, they shook their heads. The youth's neck was broken in three places, and he appeared to be paralyzed from head to foot.

They treated him for shock, wrapped him warmly in blankets, and rushed him under police escort to the Deaconess Hospital in Boston. There, the boy was subjected to an exhausting series of examinations. Hundreds of reflex tests could prove only one thing: Glen Fowler, at the age of seventeen, had been changed into a useless quadriplegic. A large nerve at the base of his neck leading from the central nervous system was severed beyond repair. This prevented any brain messages from reaching his four limbs.

Glen remained on his back for five painful months, strapped with weights and splints. With most of his body already dead, he prayed that the rest of him would not live. Gradually, he began to mistrust both himself and God and withdrew completely from all contacts with the outside world.

Alarmed over his weakening condition, the doctors at Deaconess decided to transfer Glen to the Massachusetts Hospital School in Canton. Here, he was placed under a strenuous program of occupational and physiotherapy. But he showed no desire to help himself, and his condition grew worse.

One day an attractive nurse named Joanne Rogers walked into his room. "Hello, grouchy!" she said cheerfully.

He did not reply. When he looked into her smiling face and saw how her eyes danced to an inner vitality, it made him bitterly resentful.

"Are you going to stay in that bed the rest of your life?" Joanne teased. When again he did not answer, she stepped out of his room momentarily and came back with a wheelchair. "Come," she said, "you and I are taking a spin together."

But Glen wanted no part of that wheelchair. He closed his eyes and tried to slump back into his bed until she left the room. However, Joanne did not give up. She came back the next day—and the next. Each time, she placed the wheelchair at the base of Glen's bed. Finally, on an impulse to please her, he agreed to try it. While Joanne held him firmly under the armpits, he managed to slide from the edge of his bed into the wheelchair. It was a long and tedious task, but Joanne did not seem to mind. Time ticked off a year while she cajoled, scolded and encouraged him. Slowly, he began to like the chair—grudgingly at first, then with a warming sense of looking forward to the routine.

Now the first step was over. The desire to live had been resurrected within his heart, but there still remained a more difficult obstacle to be overcome: a lack of interest in any occupation.

While in high school, Glen had shown a remarkable aptitude for art. He had won several awards and his work was rapidly recognized in North Shore art circles at the time of the accident. But that was all part of the past, Glen reminded himself as he closed his mind to his dreams of becoming a great painter. In his despair he rejected an unjust God who first gave him a talent and then took it away.

One day, deep in the throes of melancholy, he suddenly experienced an overwhelming urge to express his feelings in the one way he knew—on canvas. He asked one of the doctors for a brush and paints.

When the materials were brought into his room and

placed on his bed, the air seemed charged with tension. The doctor helped Glen into his wheelchair and watched silently as the young patient strained to pick up one of the brushes. Every muscle in his warped body tugged and pulled in an effort to grip the brush in his fingers —but it was hopeless.

The doctor moved close to Glen. He took the brush and held it before his eyes and, with no trace of pity in his voice, said, "Glen, this isn't as bad as it seems to you at the moment. I realize that you have no strength left in your arms—but from the neck up, you are strong."

"Do you expect me to paint with my neck?" Glen asked rebelliously.

"With your teeth, Glen, your *teeth!*" the doctor said.

Glen tried to laugh, but even this pained him. "You've had your fun for today, Doc," he snapped. "Now go away and leave me alone!"

The doctor persisted. "Glen, this is not a joke— believe me. There is no difference between controlling a brush with your fingers and doing the same thing with your teeth. In fact, you can get a firmer grip with your teeth."

"So you want me to paint with my teeth?" Glen's attempt at a laugh was bitter.

"Glen, do you think that God's gift to you is limited to your fingers?" the doctor asked as he touched him gently on the arm. "An artist is great, not in his fingers, but in his *heart and soul.*"

The doctor left the room then, and his words began to burn their way into Glen's mind. When he was certain that he was alone, he bent toward the bed and seized one of the brushes in his teeth. Moving his head awkwardly, he dipped it into a small container of red paint and with slow, painful strokes began to paint. There was something desperate and frightening in the wild dashes of red—but the work was his own, *his very own!*

Taking a deep breath, he reached for another brush and a fresh piece of paper. This time, he was careful and patient. He worked with deliberation and determination, even stopping several times to clean his brushes. Finally, he leaned back exhausted but happy, and viewed his first painting. It was crude and uneven, but it vibrated with meaning—a quiet pastoral scene with mountains and a stream and colorful trees lay before him.

Glen was now ready to go home. After five years in the hospital, his first concern was how to pay off the enormous bills from the hospital and the doctors. His father's salary at the Navy Yard was scarcely adequate to feed and clothe a wife and four younger children, let alone cope with $10,000 in medical expenses.

Fortunately, accident insurance would cover almost half of the bill, but that still left more than $5,000 to cast its shadows on Glen's already overburdened mind. On an impulse, he decided to enroll at the Famous Artists School in Westport, Connecticut. After submitting a few of his drawings, he was granted a full three-year scholarship, and *hope* opened its compassionate arms to welcome him.

Glen held his first exhibition before he had completed his work at the art school. When the show closed, he had sold over twenty paintings for a total of $1,200.

This was but a starter for other sales to follow. Within a matter of months, 150 of his paintings had been purchased. He was soon able to meet not only his own medical bills but also to free his family from debt.

Many honors and awards have come to this young man since then. And not the least of these is a charming wife—the devoted Joanne Rogers who first encouraged him to return to life in a hospital ward. They were married in Glen's family home in Newburyport in 1958, then moved to Beverly, Massachusetts, where Joanne works the three-to-seven shift at the local hospital.

"I am a happy man," Glen says. "Not only am I fulfilling the work that I was meant to do, but I have regained my faith in God and in myself."

Al Capp, famed cartoonist, and others share with you their own personal philosophy about . . .

VICTORY OVER HANDICAPS!

by CURTIS W. CASEWIT

Not long ago, an American newspaper sent me to the Austrian Tyrol, where I watched a unique ski race. The mountain near Innsbruck was one long garland of flags, and through the gates, at intervals of three minutes, descended a succession of skiers. They were clocked at an average of fifty miles per hour.

Nothing unusual? Not for the ordinary ski racer.

But these men were not ordinary. Twenty of them had only one leg. Fifteen others had only one arm. Three had no hands. The rest flew down the mountain despite paralyzed joints, missing kneecaps, absent toes or stiffened backs. All the skiers had handicaps—the result of war injuries or industrial accidents or previous mishaps.

These men showed me a positive mental attitude in action. Their minds had "conceived and believed" that they could ski, giving wings to their minds and strength to their bodies. Eyes shining, cheeks glowing, the racers sped through the finish line.

When the race was over, the mayor of Innsbruck handed a trophy to the three speediest skiers. Then he said simply, "You three won this annual race. But actually, all you eighty men were winners. You won over your handicaps."

The victory was not an easy one.

Skiing requires perfect co-ordination and flawless balance. To hurtle down a snowy slope, a skier needs all his limbs—his feet to direct the two wooden boards; his hands and arms to hold the ski poles which act as stabilizers.

The loss of an arm will throw a skier's body out of kilter. With only one ski pole, or "stick" as the Austrians call it, the skier will have trouble making his turns, or trying to get up a hill. Yet where there's a will, there's a way, and practice and determination will make a one-armed skier as good as a two-armed one.

The loss of a leg is much more serious; indeed, the loss will bring despair to any man. He will feel incomplete. At first, there will be pain; and when the leg has healed, he will feel off-balance. Then come the hard weeks of learning the use of crutches. The amputee will find that his remaining leg can hardly handle the load; his leg muscles will ache for several weeks. And there's the self-consciousness. But only at first. A positive mental attitude will put a man onto the right track within a few months. He'll realize that he can do many things despite a handicap.

Some of these things are sports. And the right track for some men is the ski track. Snow and faith in himself certainly did wonders for a skier named Bruno Wintersteller, who lives in Gmunden, Austria.

Bruno was a well-known ski-racer until he crashed against a tree in 1948. The leg injury was so bad that the limb had to be amputated. But Bruno knew that sun and snow and swooshing down a trail gave him the most joy despite danger and injury. So he conceived the idea that he would ski again. Wherever he went—to the small church in Gmunden, or to his factory job—Bruno's mind thought of the problems involved.

At the first snowfall, Bruno Wintersteller bought himself some special equipment—one regular ski, plus two poles fitted with tiny skis—and clambered up the wintry hills near Gmunden. He fell often and his arms hurt from so much extra work, but before he knew it, he had his old balance again. By leaning forward and using his crutch skis as brakes and steering wheels, Bruno could once more descend the trails. Each ski run made the blood tingle in his body, and sent a new wave of hope and encouragement to his brain.

"I knew I had to compete again," Bruno told me in Innsbruck. He had heard about the yearly *Versehrten-wettkämpfe,* or handicapped races, and he decided to start training. His decision paid off: twenty-four-year-old Bruno won the race for three years in a row.

Apart from skiing, Bruno is a capable mountain climber. He has conquered eighty Alpine peaks of over four thousand meters and two hundred others exceeding three thousand meters—all on one leg. He climbs every summer, leading two-legged companions up the Matterhorn, Mont Blanc and the Grossglockner. For the first few hours of each ascent, Bruno uses his regular pair of crutches, but when the rock grows steep, the one-legged mountaineer climbs with a rope. "Bruno is excellent," says Rudi Scholz, another handicapped sportsman, who has often climbed with Wintersteller. To jump across the crevasses, Bruno uses a special set of ski poles. He has also designed hand-crampons which help him up the icy stretches.

Bruno's courage has inspired countless other amputees in Europe.

After seeing Bruno and his friends—Rudi Scholz, who skis on a wooden leg; Toni Berger, who gets down the mountain on *two* artificial shins; and Erich Pletzer, who has no arms—I traveled to the Wallberg in Bavaria. Here I watched Ernst Müller, a one-legged ski instructor teaching classes of two-legged ladies. Like over one hundred thousand other Germans, Müller had lost his leg during World War II.

The shrapnel that demolished his leg did not destroy his mind. Müller believed, then achieved.

Belief comes easily to a minister like the Reverend Don Rogers, of the First Christian Church in Eugene, Oregon.

"I lost my leg as the result of a football injury," he says. But to gain self-confidence, Rogers immediately took up gymnastics and was rewarded with success on the flying rings.

When winter came, he started to ski despite his amputation and lack of previous experience. "Skiing on one leg is easier than on two," chuckles the minister. "The trouble with two skis is that they don't go in the same direction for the beginner!"

Not all handicapped persons want to ski. Some of them like to hike or use the trampoline.

Al Capp, the famed cartoonist, has his best fun by *ignoring* his wooden leg. "It has to shift for itself," Capp once said. "If it wants to come where I'm going, it has to follow me."

The cartoonist now considers his wooden leg a "useful, rather good-looking gadget," no different from a sports car or a pair of suspenders. While he stumbled and limped hard at first, he finds that in time, people forget that he is handicapped, just as they forget the color of one's eyes. Capp lost his leg back in 1919 when he was run over by a New Haven trolley car.

Will the loss of an arm bring loss of hope, too? "The contrary is true!" says Adi Hofbauer, a one-armed skier, who often competes with his friend Wintersteller in Austria. "After mastering the lack of the arm, I felt all the stronger, all the more sure of myself—on skis as well as in life."

Adi attributes his success to resolution, determination and the use of sports.

Sports and will power helped Ron Scott win a victory over his handicap. Before being drafted into the Korean war, Ron was a squash player. A Chinese sniper shot away his right arm. Now he plays with the left one. The sport has kept him in good shape ever since, just as those Austrians are in top form through physical exercises. But first of all, they had to *want* victory.

Another proof of the success of a positive mental attitude has been shown by an attractive young woman named Tomi Keitlen. She still has her legs and arms, but she is blind. Her autobiography, *Farewell to Fear*, was finished recently.

Tomi lost her sight after a series of operations when she was thirty-two years old. But she believed in herself and decided to conquer her handicap. Today she swims, plays golf, takes care of her daughter and keeps house.

She even climbs mountains by having the guide dictate her route into a tape recorder which he passes down to her. Tied to the guide by a rope, she will follow his directions: "Move your right foot about four inches to the left—now up until you feel a ledge—

now shift your weight—move your left foot out and up as far as you can go."

Tomi Keitlen claims that blindness actually helps her to climb: she feels no fear of the depths since she can't look down. Besides, as a blind person, she is in the habit of moving slowly and steadily.

But most amazing of all, Tomi learned to ski. She simply equipped her instructor with a little bell, which he rings at every dip in the mountain. In her book, she tells of making the eight-mile cross-country trip from Klosters to Davos in Switzerland.

What with her successes as a skier and climber, the choice of Tomi's occupation seems logical enough. She assists one of America's best known physical educators, Bonnie Prudden.

If you're handicapped—don't give up. Give sports a try!

6 MIND UNLIMITED

It is the mind that maketh good or ill,
that maketh wretch or happy, rich
or poor.
                                        —Edmund Spenser

*Here's the secret of preparing your mind
to achieve any goal you set for yourself.*

THE SUREST WAY IN THE WORLD
TO ATTRACT SUCCESS—
OR FAILURE

by HAROLD SHERMAN

"You might know this would happen to me!"

Is this a comment you have made, not once, but many times, when things have gone wrong? It's human nature to feel, when something unhappy has happened, that it may happen again. Your fear of it may cause you to picture the possibility of its recurrence and, without realizing it, you have set forces in motion to attract similar conditions to you. Then, when face to face with another unpleasant experience, you testify to the fact that you have anticipated it, have even helped create it by saying, "You might know this would happen to me!"

Certainly—you *knew* it was going to happen—and it did. Your *faith* in "things going wrong" caused the "power of TNT" within you to work *against* you instead of *for* you.

There is a great law of mind by which your thinking and your conduct should always be guided: "Like attracts like."

Think good thoughts; you will eventually attract good things. Think bad thoughts, you will ultimately attract bad thoughts.

Simple—easy to remember—but also easy to forget.

Even though you know the consequences of harboring destructive, apprehensive emotions—when fear and worry assail you—don't you often permit them to exist within your consciousness? We all do.

That's why our prayers for deliverance from a difficult or distressing situation are not answered.

You must *prepare* your mind to *receive* that for which you are asking before you can attract it to you —before the God Power within can help bring it to you!

How is this done? By giving the God Power the right mental pictures to work with—reinforced by your faith in God as well as in yourself.

Check back now on some of your prayers that were not answered. How did you *feel* at the time—what were your *thoughts?* Did you *picture* clearly and calmly and confidently, in your mind's eye, what you wanted the God Power to help attract to you? Or through fear did you keep on picturing the trouble you were in? If you did, then these very pictures only intensified your trouble, made it more a part of you.

Every time your "voice of fear" talks to you while you are praying, pouring such hopeless, negative thoughts into your consciousness as: "Prayer won't do any good; you can't get out of this fix; it's going to be worse tomorrow," you can be sure that your troubles will not be relieved.

There is great truth in the old, old saying: "God helps those who help themselves."

The surest way in the world to attract trouble is to *picture* the possibility of more trouble coming to you!

This isn't helping yourself or helping the God Power to help you. When an architect draws a blueprint of a house, if he makes some mistakes in calculation or design, they will show up in the finished building because the builder will faithfully and unquestioningly follow the blueprint. The architect is supposed to know his business. If the construction turns out to be wrong or weak, the architect is the one who must bear the responsibility.

You are supposed to know what you want in life. If your feelings get mixed up, through fear or worry, if you are indecisive, lacking in confidence or faith, judgment or experience, you won't be able to picture yourself *doing* or *being* or *having* the right things in your future and, as a consequence, your "power of TNT" within will be given the wrong blueprints to work on.

Get this point clearly in mind: You supply the material (by the nature of your thoughts) out of which your creative power builds your future. If the material is inferior, comprised of mental pictures of failure, despair, defeat and the like, you can readily see that only unhappy results can be materialized from them.

If you are anticipating the worst while hoping for the best, you will get the worst. The things that happen to you are in direct accordance with the things wherein you place your faith. Believe you are licked —and you are. Your belief instructs the Power Within to produce failure.

Trouble is the product of wrong thinking. Straighten out your thinking and your troubles must vanish. They cannot continue to exist because they have been created and kept alive by wrong thinking—and a change of mental attitude always brings about a change of conditions and experiences.

You cannot think love and hate at the same time— either one or the other must dominate. So it is with every constructive or destructive feeling. There is a continuous battle going on in our consciousness for the ascendancy of good and bad feelings. As creatures

of free will and free choice, it is up to us to develop
and maintain emotional control. It is our job to conquer our fears and worries, our likes and dislikes, and
to direct our desires into right channels. Once we do
this, we begin to get right results in every department
of our lives; things commence to happen as they should
happen; success becomes a regular pattern, in place
of failure.

The admonition: "Don't trouble trouble 'til trouble
troubles you," is a good one. Because you have had
an unfortunate experience is no indication that this
experience need be repeated in your future—unless
you start brooding about it, fearing its repetition, even
inviting it by a continued picture of a like occurrence.

Your feelings are dynamite. They have the power
to make or break you. Take inventory of your feelings
this very minute—about others, about your problems,
your future. Are you worried, apprehensive, resentful,
fearful, when you should be relaxed, self-confident,
in good spirits, filled with courage and faith?

Whatever conditions you are facing at the moment
are the result of your past thinking—good and bad.
These conditions cannot change until you have first
changed your thinking.

Do you wish to attract more trouble? You can easily
do it! Just persist in maintaining a wrong mental attitude toward someone or some experience. That's all
you need to do, and you'll see how quickly and posi-
tively this power within will serve you—in reverse.

Remember—you are the architect and this "power
of TNT" is the builder. It operates like a magnet, attracting to you what you picture.

Things first happen in your mind before they can
happen in this outer world. What are you picturing?
Do you want it to happen? If not, you are the only

one who can prevent it. Your future success or failure is in your hands—where it should be.

Don't ever say again: "You might know this would happen to me!" Say instead: "I know only Good is going to happen to me—because my thinking is right."

The greatest and most intricate electronic computer ever built will never approach the capability of your mind.

YOUR SOURCE OF POWER

by NAPOLEON HILL

Of all the great men I have known, Thomas A. Edison intrigued me most. Perhaps this was due to the fact that despite his lack of formal education he became the foremost man of achievement in the field of the sciences.

I was intrigued also because of the mental attitude in which Mr. Edison related himself to his affliction of deafness. When I asked him if he had not found his work very difficult because of his deafness, he replied: "To the contrary, deafness has been a great help to me. It has saved me from having to listen to a lot of worthless chatter from men who did not know what they were talking about, and it has taught me to *hear from within*."

The latter part of that statement is very significant, especially to the person who is seeking the way to peace of mind through understanding of self. By transmuting his affliction into a positive mental attitude, Mr. Edison learned how to tune in on Infinite Intelligence and get his knowledge from an infallible source.

Thomas A. Edison was far and away the calmest man I have ever known. He had no frustration complexes. He had no fears. He had no regrets about anything or anyone. He had no grandiose ideas of his own importance, but he did have humility of the heart, which made him truly great.

His understanding of the benefits of closing the door behind disappointing experiences was profoundly reflected in the fact that before he perfected the incandescent electric light, he met with more than ten thousand separate and distinct failures. Think of a mind which is capable of setting a goal, and then letting nothing turn it aside until that goal is reached, and you have a perfect picture of the quality which made Mr. Edison great.

Once I asked Mr. Edison, "What would you have done if you had not finally uncovered the secret of the incandescent electric lamp?"

With a merry twinkle in his eyes he replied: "I would be in my laboratory working now, instead of wasting my time talking with you."

Mr. Edison knew no such reality as "failure" because he had discovered the supreme secret which leads to peace of mind and understanding of the source and power of the mind. Without the aid of that supreme secret, Mr. Edison never would have become the world's number one inventor.

Because of his knowledge of the supreme secret, Thomas A. Edison carried on through more than ten thousand definite failures in his search for the solution of a problem. I wonder how many people know the number of failures the average man can survive without quitting and giving up the ghost in despair. To satisfy my curiosity on this subject I once made a survey through which I examined men and women to ascertain their staying qualities in the face of failure or defeat.

The majority of them quit trying when overtaken one time by defeat. A very small percentage of them kept on trying a second time. But by far the greater number quit even before meeting with defeat because they expected it and quit before they really started.

Needless to suggest, there were no Edisons and no Fords in this group.

They were the average run-of-the-mill of humanity who somehow never got around to recognizing the master key to riches with which they were endowed at birth: a master key consisting of their ability to tune in and appropriate the powers of Infinite Intelligence by the simple process of conditioning their minds to receive and use this great universal power.

I have observed two important facts concerning men who are successful in their chosen occupations and those who are not. The successes speak in the future tense of yet unattained objectives which they intend to achieve. The failures speak in the past tense, of their defeats and their disappointments. I have never known the rule to fail.

I have observed another trait concerning successes and failures. The successful man usually speaks in complimentary terms of other men who are succeeding, while the failure usually has a word of criticism of the men who are succeeding.

Envy and revenge are very ugly words. More ugly still is the character of the person who indulges in these emotions. They represent emotions against which the doors of one's mind must be tightly closed if one is to enjoy peace of mind.

The source of Mahatma Gandhi's influence over

more than a hundred million of his followers was a great mystery to many people. They could not understand how a man who had no money, no military equipment, no organized soldiers could defy the powerful British Government and so successfully get away with it.

What was the source of Gandhi's power? He simply mobilized the mind-power of more than a hundred million people, who fixed their minds upon the major objective of routing the British and freeing India. Time turned this purpose into action which forced the British to withdraw. *Remember, organized mind-power is greater than organized military power.*

Note, however, this important feature of the Gandhi mind-power. He freed his mind of all desire for revenge, all hatred, all desire for personal aggrandizement. He sought no robes of honor for himself; nor did he seek any form of material riches. All he sought was the privilege of mobilizing the mind-power of the Indian people for the purpose of gaining their freedom from British rule.

There is something profound about the powers of a man who moves under this type of impersonal motive. There is something truly great about the man who seeks freedom and benefits for others, while he seeks nothing for himself but the privilege of serving. Perhaps this "something," whatever it is, was responsible for the success of George Washington's armies when they were fighting against great odds, for the independence of this nation.

Close the doors of your mind to everything which causes you anxiety, fear, envy, greed and the desire of something for nothing. The penalty for failure to close the doors will be loss of the peace of mind which you are seeking.

Through no fault of your own, you lost your job.

There are two moves you can make. First, you can nurse your wounded feelings until they fester into resentment and hatred of your former employer. In that frame of mind you will find it extremely difficult to get another job, no matter how skilled in your occupation you may be. No employer wants a person with a negative mind around any place of business. He has a bad effect on the customers and the other employees.

Secondly, you can transmute your temporary frustration into a determined will to get a better job than the one you lost, close the door on your old job and start right where you stand to find just the job you desire. If you speak of your former employer at all, be sure to speak of him in complimentary terms. That may not help him any, but it will do *you* a lot of good.

You have been injured, perhaps unjustly, by someone who works with you in your occupation. Here you are face to face with an opportunity to learn whether or not you have within you the makings of bigness. If you are potentially a great person, you will forgive and close the door behind you on the incident.

If you have not the foundation for greatness, you will find ways and means of striking back at the person who injured you, and possibly go so far as to cause that person to lose his job. In that event you will be the more unfortunate person of the two, for truly any person who expresses any form of revenge is unfortunate. Revenge is like a boomerang. It often comes back to wound the person who sets it into motion against another.

You have held your present position for a long while without getting the promotions to which you believe you are entitled. There are two things you can do about it. First, you can open wide the doors to your mind so that Old Man Grudge can enter and make you grouchy. In that event, you may never get the promotions you desire, but you will be almost sure to "get the gate" sooner or later.

Secondly, you can start right where you stand and apply the habit of going the extra mile by rendering more service and better service than you are now being paid for, and doing it in a pleasing mental attitude. By this method, and this method alone, you can make yourself so valuable that your employer cannot afford to keep you in your present job, but he will voluntarily move you up into another station. If he is so lacking in imagination as not to recognize your better type of service, then someone else may recognize it and your reward may come from an entirely different source.

When it comes to the entertainment of anger or hurt feelings, remember they, also, are to be put behind that closed door. It is most important for you to know that no one may make you angry or hurt your feelings in any manner whatsoever, *without your willing co-operation*.

Your state of mind is something you can control completely. And you may be surprised to learn, after you become better acquainted with this "door closing" idea, how easily you can take possession of your mind and condition it for the attainment of any purpose you desire.

No one can control the actions of others, or many of the circumstances of life which tend to make one angry, *but anyone may control his reactions to these actions and circumstances*. Your mind is your own. You are the sole supervisor of its reactions to every circumstance which affects your life. Learn to close the door of your mind and shut out the negative reactions if you wish to find peace of mind and lasting prosperity.

One of the world's foremost psychiatrists helps you to re-evaluate your whole personality.

ARE YOU EMOTIONALLY MATURE?

by DR. WILLIAM C. MENNINGER

It is always helpful to have a little honest self-inspection. Now and then we should try to brush away a few of the cobwebs of conceit, arrogance and prejudice that all of us have and see ourselves by a set of standards that perhaps would help us to grow emotionally.

The need to grow up emotionally is vital for each of us. To be emotional is a part of the life of all of us. Often it's the part of us that makes us do foolish things and occasionally it makes us do fine things, but in any event emotional maturity is related directly to good mental health.

It's a curious fact that no one has been able to define mental health satisfactorily. Everyone agrees that it is much more than the absence of illness and thus emotional maturity, in a sense, is much more than the lack of immaturity. Your emotions are just one facet of that complicated thing called your personality. In your total psychological life there are many facets such as the intellectual aspect, the social and others that we can measure as to their degree of effectiveness and maturity, and we have discovered that theoretically any of these aspects of your personality can mature alongside of another aspect that doesn't mature. In other words, you may mature in one direction and yet show great immaturity in another.

For example, we often encounter the intellectual genius with a very high IQ who actually is a social blacksmith. He can't get along with people even though he is so brilliant that he makes the rest of us a little uncomfortable because of his brilliance. There is the successful businessman who is a genius in terms of his business and yet he is a flop as a father. There is the meticulous housewife who keeps her home so spic and span that it's a little uncomfortable to be in and yet, unfortunately, she doesn't know how to make love. These are all curious mixtures where the individual is so outstanding, effective and mature in one area and yet obviously immature in other ways.

I have selected seven potential yardsticks for measuring your emotional maturity although there are more. As you read, be honest with yourself, and perhaps you will form ideas that will help you change your personality—and your life.

1. Deal Constructively with Reality.

There is much selfishness, suspicion, hostility, lack of understanding, witch hunting, dishonesty and violence in the world we live in. That's reality. Now it's quite normal for small children and very seriously ill mental patients to ignore reality and although we all try to run from it now and then, most of the time we must stand and face it . . . and sometimes it gets rough. It is under these circumstances that I wonder how you behave and how you play your game of life. Many of us take no responsibility for the cards that are dealt them even though they selected the game. It is in this general area that we can measure people by how they react to a situation that causes them a great deal of frustration.

One of the most difficult lessons that you had to learn as a child was how to accept delay and many of us go through life with the infantile principle of getting what we want when we want it or we'll let loose all hell. There are many who cannot accept frustration and yet reality is such that one cannot live without often being frustrated.

When the going gets rough, how does one maintain his own sense of personal security? By what means, by what kinds of support? There is an internal kind of security that is essential for each of us ... a serenity that is significant whether we are mature or not. In many this is conspicuously absent.

There is also a need for external security ... a sense of feeling that we are needed, wanted, and loved. Nothing in our social order is more disastrous than to be "black-balled" or rejected as a child or as an adult.

I believe emotional maturity implies that you do not run when the going gets rough nor do you react by destructive fighting. To deal constructively with reality requires a philosophy, a set of attitudes and perhaps a way of living that will fortify you against the "buzz saws" that you meet each day. Develop an attitude that is concerned with your aspirations, hopes and determination for the future, rather than the past. Tell yourself, "I'm making the most of my situation. I can complain about it, I can handle it in many immature ways, but I am a mature person and I will meet the situation with what I have and what I can do." Learn to live without certainty and yet without being overwhelmed by the anxieties that surround us all the time.

2. Have the Capacity to Change.

The only certain thing in life these days is constant

change. The world is changing and so are we, daily ... almost hourly. The other day I heard a story about a top IBM man. Ten years ago he worked all summer on a special set of problems. When the first major computer came out, it took six hours to solve these same problems. Then it was revised and these problems took just six minutes. Now it takes less than a second to do the job that once took all summer.

We, if we are going to mature, must learn to live with these changes and make the most of them. Parents, especially, must learn to accept challenges and changes. They cannot expect to run their children as they themselves were brought up. It's a different world. We have a monster that sits over in the corner of the living room, you know, and that, in most cases, pretty nearly destroys family life. There have been many changes in the past twenty-five years and yet I still see parents who refuse to change or to grow with their children. There are still too many people who go through life by hammering on the desk and wanting what they want, when they want it, because they won't change and they won't grow up.

Many don't want a new experience of any kind and when they have one, they don't quite know how to handle it. They fail to learn from experience and so they don't grow. They keep using old techniques and they keep failing.

The individual addicted to alcohol repeats and repeats the same experience without ever learning that he has a fatal allergy for a substance that he mustn't try to handle, but there are many adults, not alcoholics, who get in ruts and in one way or another, hurt themselves because they don't get out of the rut.

There are other compulsions besides alcohol that make life difficult for many, and one's capacity to change by replacing bad habits with good ones is another measure of the emotionally mature person.

3. Be Free of Tension and Anxiety Symptoms.

All of us are at times unreasonable, irrational and often quite illogical. These are what we call neurotic evasions. Some individuals are too aggressive, others respond with conceit, many are too passive, too fearful, too lonesome, but whatever characteristic they assume it is a device that they utilize to get along and we should recognize it. There are individuals who always have to be fifteen minutes early and there are others that always must be fifteen minutes late. Some empty ash trays at the first trace of an ash, and others seem to "enjoy" worrying . . . worrying about anything.

Our emotions can give us any kind of physical symptom in the book from a peptic ulcer to high blood pressure. These are things we can't control ourselves and, of course, there is the "tension headache." Television has educated us on what to do about these headaches, but it hasn't discussed the causes. They are emotional responses and some people thrive on them—including the aspirin people.

Remember the GIs and their "aching backs"? Less than 5 per cent of the backs showed anything organically wrong. The fact remains that these aches and pains are often an automatic device in our personality resulting from our frustrating attempts to solve specific problems in our life.

Another neurotic evasion that many of us use is to blame someone else. My wife tells me that probably the best advantage of marriage is that you've got a "scapegoat." It's the other partner's fault when you're late or when the buttons don't get sewed on. We rationalize many of our actions with our families and in our business, and some good evidence of our maturity is being able to recognize this fault in ourselves.

One other word about tensions and anxieties so that I am not misunderstood. I believe we all need a little tension and anxiety. I hope we all have a little bit of restlessness, whether you choose to call it "noble discontent," "righteous indignation" or the anxiety to do things when we see they ought to be done. We all need some motivation but when your anxiety climbs to the point where a tension headache results, then there is a maladjustment.

4. Find More Satisfaction from Giving Than Getting.

One criterion of the well-adjusted person is the capacity to find more satisfaction out of giving than out of getting. We all started as infants on the receiving end of the line, but we truly become an emotionally mature adult when our satisfaction is in giving without reflection on "What's in it for me?" Good mental health for the most mature person is finding a "cause" . . . the earlier in life the better . . . and the bigger the better. Try to find a cause so big that you can work at it enthusiastically and hard all your life. Psychiatry bears out an old admonition. "If you really want to save your life . . . lose it." If you don't have some mission in life, it's later than you think. Find the mission and you will find happiness.

5. Relate to People.

The mature person can consistently maintain relationships with people. There is much evidence around us of failures in human relationships. How do you treat your children? Do you reject them one time and accept them another? Are you too busy to spend time with them? From the individual family to the world in general, we just aren't getting along with each other very well. We just don't want to get along together and, of course, our international philosophy suggests that, if worst comes to worst, the only way to settle an argument is to shoot the other person. We now spend $52 billion a year preparing for this, yet we know full well that if we ever started it, we'd all be gone . . . and there wouldn't be anybody to call us out of those shelters they want to build.

A mature relationship depends on many things that no psychological test ever measured in any of us. How does a person become sincere . . . and how do you measure his sincerity? Often you can sense sincerity in another person, but some of us are shams and we show it while others always have their cards "face up," are honest, have convictions . . . and are willing to stand and be counted.

How do we learn integrity and measure it? How do we acquire that combination of honesty and fairness, dependability and willingness to assume responsibility so that people can count on us? Usually you can sense these qualities in others. You can feel it. Hopefully we can also try to assess these in ourselves . . . with honesty.

6. Control Your Hostile Impulses.

All of us were born with hostile feelings and impulses. When we recognize them, we have a much better chance to handle them before we turn these hostile expressions on ourselves. Whenever we get a guilt feeling it's because we've been forgetful, thoughtless, nasty or hostile toward someone. We then turn this feeling on ourself in various types of self-defeatism. Often we refuse to let ourself succeed, but we do not understand the reasons for our failure. Many of us go around with a lack of confidence which is still another method of turning aggressiveness on one's self. Some of us go through rituals of self-punishment and, of course, the ultimate man turns hate on himself, which is suicide. Then he goes all the way and kills himself.

Frequently we turn our hate on our family without even being aware of it. There are many disguises for hostility toward the spouse or the children, such as shunning responsibilities, running out, neglect, thoughtlessness, rejection, unfaithfulness and forgetfulness. All of these things we do in varying degrees to each other . . . to people we love. We should learn to recognize these actions when we do them. There is a wonderful adage, "Love thy neighbor as thyself," but all of us love ourselves far, far too much to reach that ideal point. But it has its psychiatric implications. It's an ideal that any of us, in terms of maturity, should be aiming for every day of our lives.

7. Love.

The most important measurement of your emotional maturity is how much you can love. Your capacity to care about other people in the broadest sense is this business of love.

We began in infancy completely dependent upon our parents. If we were fortunate, the Almighty gave us parents that really cared about us. They loved us and we learned to love in return. As we grow we form relations with other people, our playmates, our schoolmates and our college companions. Eventually we find somebody we truly care about and we extend our capacity to care to someone of the opposite sex. Ultimately we become a family which is the richest reward any of us can have.

Gradually we extend our interests and our capacity to care to the neighborhood, the community, the state, the nation and the shrinking world which should be the concern of every mature person. Now our love has reached its fullest potential. I use love here to personify the constructive forces of life that got a start in each of us.

Hate can only flourish where love is absent. The only neutralization for hate is love and only as we can learn to love enough can we control the hate that seems to pervade so much of life today. Therefore, it seems to me, the most important goal for any of us to aim at, regardless of our age, is an increase in our capacity to be interested in others, to be concerned with others, to give to others, to care for others, to love others. Love is the pre-eminent characteristic of the emotionally mature person.

Intuition is an incredible power of the mind that you can develop to improve your business and personal life.

FOLLOW YOUR HUNCHES

by FRANK L. REMINGTON

Years ago I met a girl at a dinner party. A strong feeling about her swept through me. "What a wonderful person," an inner voice seemed to whisper. My hunch proved to be sound. For she became my wife and I still feel the same way about her.

One morning last week when leaving the house, a feeling of uneasiness passed over me. "Don't close the door yet," something seemed to warn me. Casually I walked back into the front room. There on the table lay my house keys where I'd tossed them. Had I closed the door I'd have been locked out.

As a writer, I've often experienced hunches about my work. Ideas for stories have popped into my mind "right out of the blue." And I've usually found them excellent subjects for development.

Doubtless you've many times experienced a sudden discernment about someone or something. And more often than not, this unexpected insight proved to be correct. You congratulated yourself for your sage "guessing," dismissing one of your most remarkable mental faculties: intuition.

What is intuition? Can it be cultivated and help in your everyday living? Psychologists say intuition can be cultivated—that it is a normal but little-used mental function. Even the savants, however, don't know all the answers, for the remarkable powers of the human mind have scarcely been fathomed by researchers.

Intuition has been defined as "a wordless thinking and a shortcut to truth—the tapping of unconscious memories and senses that civilization has blunted." It is also the faculty of knowing something without knowing why.

Although your brain weighs but two and one-half pounds, it files away incredible amounts of information. It is estimated that your nervous system sends about ten thousand bits of information to your brain every second, or close to fifteen trillion impulses during a lifetime. It records and remembers everything that has ever entered your experience: every incident, every thought, every smell, every word.

At a given moment your conscious mind can recall only about 10 per cent of this incalculable amount of data. The rest lies buried in your subconscious mind, usually beyond recall. In hypnosis or in dreams some of this information comes through. But it is usually jumbled because the conscious mind is asleep.

Many bits of data long forgotten can be recalled by the subconscious and brought to the surface of your conscious mind. Sometimes, when you can't remember a specific fact, date or name, you pass the question to your subconscious with the silent command: "Recall this name for me." In a few moments, or a few hours, *pop!* comes the name. This is a marvelous demonstration of the mental processes at work for us at the subconscious level.

When encouraged, the subconscious uses its prodigious store of knowledge that you never knew you had to solve vexing problems—problems that the conscious mind cannot even comprehend. When your subconscious works for you this way, you usually declare: "The idea just came to me," or "I have a hunch." The idea and the impulse both stemmed from your inner mind.

If you've been married long, you've probably developed the knack of sometimes "reading" your wife's mind or knowing your husband's next move. Over the years, you've gotten to know your spouse so well that a fleeting expression, a certain tone of voice, the flutter of an eyelid or the tightening of a muscle will telegraph what he or she is going to say or do.

Actually, you don't "read" these signs consciously. You simply get a hunch without knowing how it originated. But if you act on it you'll usually be right.

Intuition originates hunches, and it is always based on knowledge acquired through the years. The person whose hunches are consistently correct usually is well informed in the field to which his hunches relate. As Louis Pasteur observed, "Intuition is given only to him who has undergone long preparation to receive it."

Thus professional people become quite intuitive about their own line of work. A doctor, for example, can often literally "smell" a disease without examining the patient. This ability comes from long experience with the disease.

Professional weight-guessers and age-guessers at carnivals and fairs earn their livelihood through intuition. At a glance they can determine a stranger's age and weight without knowing how they do it. They've developed their intuition in this line by long years of practice and experience.

Artists, scientists, writers, inventors and composers are all guided by sudden illuminations and hunches. All truly creative activity depends in some degree on these signals from the subconscious mind.

Usually the subconscious mind works while the conscious mind is relaxing—while you're out walking, playing tennis or fast asleep. At that time, the inner mind chooses and classifies facts from your buried store of experience and knowledge and comes up with the answer.

Mozart dreamed many of his famed compositions. Voltaire composed poems while asleep and transcribed them upon awakening. Benjamin Franklin received many of his ideas from his subconscious mind while in slumber. The basic idea for the strange story of *Dr. Jekyll and Mr. Hyde* came to Robert Louis Stevenson in a dream.

It is a common misconception that some people possess a divine gift for accurate and sudden inspiration, bright ideas or hunches. Women, in particular, reputedly are so endowed. Nothing could be further from the truth.

True, women have certain intuitions which are rare among men. But there is a reason. Their mental flashes usually concern areas which women normally monopolize. Men, for instance, listen more to what people say while women tend to sense what people are feeling. The special training most women go through has made them attentive to things many males disregard almost entirely.

When the sexes' interests are the same their hunches and intuitions are similar, too, with only individual variations. When men and women have different major interests, their intuitions are different. The difference, however, rises from the nature of the interests, not from the nature of the sexes.

A hunch does not crystallize from nowhere. It comes from past experiences and deals invariably with familiar things. You kid yourself at the race track, for example, if you have hunches as to which horses will win. But a jockey, because he has grown up with horses and with racing, may have a genuine hunch.

If I almost walk out the door without my key, what is it that warns me not to close the door? My unconscious senses doubtless catch an almost imperceptible clue. Perhaps my hand, brushing against the pocket where the keys usually rest, notes their absence and telegraphs a warning to my brain.

Or maybe the missing keys lightened the weight of my pocket—not enough to be felt consciously, but sufficiently to be caught by my unconscious senses. So I have a sudden hunch and thus recover the keys.

You can develop your intuition and through it use your hunches to further your career, improve your human relationships and generally enrich your life. There are numerous steps you can take to encourage your intuition.

First of all, broaden your interests—make your brain more active. Reading good books, developing the art of conversation and cultivating a large circle of friends will help to stimulate your mind. Such activities may lead to valuable clues in unexpected fields and help to crystallize the shapeless thoughts lurking in the corners of your subconscious.

Don't rebel at new ideas. Hunches and sudden inspirations largely originate in the subconscious mind, probably because the conscious mind, bound up in age-old habits and conventions, often refuses to accept the new and strange. The broader your experience and the more open your mind, the better chance your intuition has to operate effectively.

Learn to relax. Your intuition can't operate when your conscious mind is tied in knots or cluttered with worry and anxiety. Sir Walter Scott put his intuition to work by "sleeping on it." When a problem bothered him unduly, he'd say to himself, "Never mind. I shall have the answer at seven o'clock tomorrow morning." And he usually did.

Learn to use your intuition. One famous scientist formed a habit of always keeping a pad and pencil handy at his bedside to jot down thoughts occurring in the night. Similarly, he recorded his daytime hunches on pocket memo cards.

Thomas A. Edison, when he came up against a tough problem, would fully review all the salient facts and then forget the entire matter for twenty-four hours. More often than not, the solution would pop into his mind during the day.

You can do the same. Even if the answer doesn't come, you'll see the whole problem lined up in clearer perspective when you next think about it.

As you learn to use your intuition, your hunches will become more numerous and accurate. Ultimately, they will develop in you a feeling of self-confidence which you've never before experienced. Then, as happens in so many life situations, when you must make an instant decision where your learning alone will not help you, you can play that hunch and rest upon your resulting action with calm assurance.

He frightened the stagehands when he called for . . .

THE "BIG ME"

by MARJORIE SPILLER NEAGLE

The story is told that on an opening night, before the great Enrico Caruso became famous, he was overcome by stage fright. As he stood in the wings, his throat contracted with a spasm of terror. Sweat poured from him. He was on the verge of running away.

Suddenly a thought struck him.

"The little me on the outside is strangling the big me on the inside. The me that wants to sing . . . that *can* sing . . . must come out."

He began a whispered shout. "Get out of the way! Get out! Get out!"

The stagehands looked at him frightened, and other members of the cast wondered if Caruso had taken leave of his senses.

By the time the cue came for the singer to make his entrance, the "little me" had been routed and the "big me" was in command.

After Caruso finished his aria the audience rose to its feet, cheering and shouting, "Bravo!"

A powerful force had been put into the person of Caruso. Only when he recognized that a weak force was holding it back and acted upon that knowledge, did the stronger one come through.

7 HEALTH UNLIMITED

*He who has health has hope; and he
who has hope, has everything.*
—*Arabian Proverb*

Recent medical discoveries about what happens when the mercury rises in your thermometer prove it is not always cause for alarm.

FEVER!

by JAMES C. SPAULDING

Do you reach for aspirin at the first flush of fever, or do you tend to let the ailment take its natural course?

The tendency these days among parents (and many doctors) is to consider fever an enemy, but the experts say it may be a friend. In any case, there are sound reasons to be sparing in the use of fever remedies.

An eminent physiologist and one of the foremost authorities on body temperature control, Dr. Eugene F. Du Bois, said that "Fever is only a symptom, and we are not sure it is an enemy; perhaps it is a friend."

Dr. Du Bois discovered by experimenting that body temperature rises four or five degrees during vigorous exercise or strenuous physical work. Thus you can be sure that when Herb Elliott of Australia set the present world record for the mile (three minutes, fifty-four and four-tenths seconds) he was running a temperature of 102 or 103 degrees.

Elliott was certainly not sick; his fever was normal for hard exercise.

"This throws light on fever," Dr. Du Bois said, "since athletes can make world records at body temperatures well in the fever level. Is fever beneficial?"

In the days before wonder drugs, fever used to be

prescribed for almost every ailment from the common cold to hardening of the arteries. "Sweating out" a cold is an ancient practice—and still followed to some extent today.

Fever once was the best treatment for particularly tenacious cases of venereal disease. VD organisms cannot survive temperatures much higher than 105 degrees. Fevers that high and higher used to be caused deliberately by giving the patient injections of malarial parasites or typhoid vaccine. Dr. Julius Wagner-Jauregg won a Nobel prize in 1927 for his development of fever therapy.

If you are normally healthy, you can tolerate high fever for several days. However, if your body temperature rises higher than 106 degrees, doctors consider it dangerous. There is a possibility that the temperature may rise suddenly and uncontrollably. This could lead to heat exhaustion and even death.

How high can your body temperature go? Temperatures of 130 and 150 degrees have been reported in medical journals, but these were certainly faked. Doctors say that malingering with the fever thermometer is curiously common. Some put the thermometer near a light bulb, in hot water or rub it against the bed sheet to heat it by friction.

A New York City woman, nevertheless, ran a bona fide fever higher than 110 degrees and lived. The mercury climbed past the 110 mark; her doctor estimated her temperature at 114 degrees.

Your "normal" body temperature of 98.6 degrees is just an approximation. In any day, your body temperature ordinarily varies several degrees. Usually, it is lowest just before you awake in the morning and is the highest in the late afternoon or evening.

Your children's body temperatures normally rise higher than yours and vary more. A vigorous game, an emotional upset or too much clothing—all can raise your child's temperature to the fever level.

Dr. Du Bois has advocated abolishing the little red "normal" arrow on the fever thermometer and replacing it with a normal range marking of about 97 to 100 degrees. This, said Dr. Du Bois, would spare mothers needless anxiety and the doctor needless calls.

You develop a fever when your body's heat-dissipating mechanisms cannot keep pace with heat production. For instance, doctors say it is common for parents to bring their sick child to the hospital bundled up heavily, even in warm weather, so it is no wonder the child is running several degrees of fever. The fever disappears when the extra clothing is removed.

Recent research indicates that most of the fevers you run are not caused directly by the germs of infection in your body, but by a substance certain white blood cells release in response to the germ toxins. You develop a fever when this white cell substance acts on your brain's heat-regulating centers.

If you play hard tennis for an hour, your body temperature will rise to a fever level. It will rise to the same level if you chop wood vigorously on a cold winter day. The outside temperature has little influence on the temperature inside your body in most circumstances.

You might think that if you exercised harder or if the outside temperature was hotter, your body would get hotter, too, but it doesn't. The reason is that in those circumstances, your body simply eliminates more heat. It does this by sending more hot blood through the vessels close to the surface of the skin. The skin gets rid of your excess heat by radiation and by the evaporation of perspiration, especially the latter.

If you want to check what hard exercise does to

your body temperature, better not take it by mouth. Your mouth temperature in exercise will stay "normal," or even fall slightly because of rapid breathing, which will cool your mouth.

Dr. Du Bois and his colleagues have discovered that your fever from disease is very much like your fever from exercise. Neither exceeds 105 degrees, except in rare instances.

Why not? There must be a secondary heat-regulating mechanism that is called into play when you are sick or you exercise, Dr. Du Bois said, and this extra mechanism "vigorously opposes" any tendency for your temperature to rise above about 105 degrees. If you did not have such a control, your body temperature might easily rise to fatal heights.

You may have wondered at times why you should shiver and shake while running a high fever. Experiments have shown that you experience a chill during fever when the products of infection—malarial parasites, for instance—temporarily set your body's thermostat higher.

In a chill, you do two things (besides piling on blankets) that make you hotter. Blood vessels in your skin constrict, reducing heat loss, and you shiver. Shivering may not seem like exercise, but it is. By shivering alone, you can increase the heat production of your body five or six times.

Usually the higher setting of your thermostat that brings on the chill lasts only a short while. Then the setting drops back to a lower fever level and you feel hot again. The blood floods your skin blood vessels, you perspire and soon your fever decreases.

The old saying, "Feed a cold and starve a fever" is doubtful medical advice, so far as fever is concerned. To begin with, you need more energy when you have a fever because you are using more. Your body burns its fuel seven per cent faster with each degree of rise in body temperature. If your fever is 105 degrees, your metabolism is half again as great as normal.

Unfortunately, however, your appetite almost always lags. This is not likely to be harmful from a nutritional standpoint, because you can do without food for a few days. But you cannot do without water, and solid food is your body's chief source of water. Meat is three-fourths water. Some vegetables contain a higher proportion of water than milk does.

When you are feverish you lose water faster because you sweat and exhale more water vapor. At the same time, you tend to drink less water and to eat little or nothing. As a result, you may become dehydrated, and this itself can lead to fever. Highly colored urine is a sign of dehydration. In severe form, dehydration can be harmful or even deadly.

To avoid dehydration, "feeding a fever" would be good advice. James Graves, an American physician who died in 1853, defied the old saying and fed his fever patients. He asked that his epitaph read: "He Fed Fevers."

Fever drugs (antipyretics) are "grossly overused" in the opinion of Dr. Alan K. Done, a Stanford University pediatrician. Fever of 104 or even 105 degrees for several days will not harm you, he said, unless you have heart disease or are debilitated. Children known to be susceptible to fever convulsions should not be allowed to develop fevers, either.

Aspirin, the most commonly used fever drug, will itself cause fever if taken in toxic doses.

Dr. Done said that using aspirin and other fever drugs had various disadvantages. For instance, fever may strengthen your body's defense against infection. (This has been neither proved nor refuted.)

Your fever may be a valuable clue to the severity

of the disease, to the effectiveness of treatment and to the occurrence of complications or setbacks.

The fever drug you take may suppress other symptoms besides fever. For example, the drugs may hide the rheumatic symptoms of rheumatic heart disease, while the disease process remains unchecked.

Drugs that lower your fever may simply delay obtaining a diagnosis of your disease and put off the start of the proper treatment of it.

Dr. Done thinks that the tendency to use aspirin freely when fever arises may be a contributing cause of the many cases of accidental aspirin poisoning in the home. He said that most often such poisonings occur after a parent has taken the aspirin bottle from its usual place and left it where a little child could reach it.

This does not mean that you should deny your children—or yourself—the comfort that lowering a high fever can bring. But Dr. Done said that children usually tolerate fever well. Besides, you often can bring their temperature down without using drugs. You can lower the room temperature or remove excess bed clothing, for instance.

Fever, in many cases, is not your enemy, but your ally. Treat it accordingly.

*If tension and worry are weapons you are
using to commit slow suicide, this advice
is for you.*

HOW TO LIVE LONGER

by FRANK ROSE

"The most common cause of death today is suicide."
This startling statement was made to me recently by
a doctor friend while I was interviewing him for a
health magazine.

"But, Doc," I protested, "the suicide rate isn't that
high. I have some figures on it right here." I started
groping through my briefcase. He waved his hand
impatiently.

"I know the statistics. I'm not talking about official
suicide with guns and other lethal instruments. Most
people choose a slower method. But it's just as fatal
in the long run. I'm talking about worry, pessimism
and fear. They're the greatest killers of our time!"

After this revealing interview, I spent several weeks
researching the subject. I read dozens of books,
pamphlets and magazine articles. I talked with a score
of physicians, psychologists and clergymen. All agreed
that the hectic tempo of modern living with its resultant tension is a serious national problem. All voiced
the opinion that millions of Americans are slowly killing themselves with the deadly weapon of anxiety.

As one doctor put it, "Ailments caused by negative
thinking account for more sickness than all other
diseases combined. Such sickness is not imaginary, as

many suppose. It is just as real as a broken leg and usually far more serious."

"What is the answer?" I asked.

He shrugged his shoulders. "Get people to stop worrying. Get them to relax. But don't ask me how. I don't know." He stared out of the office window for several moments with a troubled expression on his face. "Nowadays," he continued, "people always seem to be expecting the worst and that's what they usually get. They fail to realize that most of their afflictions are self-created, that negative thoughts always produce negative results. They've lost their confidence—or faith, or whatever you want to call it—that things will go well and this vital lack is short-circuiting their health and their ability to cope adequately with life's problems."

A clergyman expanded this point. "Faith is the answer, all right, but not the vague, passive attitude that usually passes by that name. Real faith is not hope or desire; it is the optimism that comes from inside. It is, above all, a creative force. It makes good things happen.

"Too many people today associate faith with purely religious activities. They don't bring its dynamic power into their workaday lives and, without it, they are ill equipped to ward off the swarms of troubles that beset us all these days. Worry stems from fear, and fear is an outright admission of lack of faith. A round-the-clock working faith is the only armor against worry and fear."

All of the persons interviewed agreed that a working faith of some kind was the solution to our growing health problem, and that the public needs to be educated to the fact that our health and happiness depend upon our mental attitude.

But how can our thoughts make us sick? To many

people this is incomprehensible. They think of their minds and emotions as something apart and totally different from their bodies. This is not true, as research and discoveries in the field of psychosomatic medicine have clearly proven. The mind and body are interrelated. What affects one affects the other.

William James, the noted psychologist, defined an emotion as "the state of mind that manifests itself by a perceptible change in the body." It is easy to verify the truth of this statement from your own experience. Remember the last time that you became angry? Were you affected only in your mind, or did your face flush, your eyes widen and your muscles tighten and tremble?

Think back to a time of fear. Do you recall the creeping sensation at the back of your neck, the lump in your throat, the tight knot in your stomach, your pounding heart? Have you ever fainted at the sight of blood? Or been sick to your stomach because of disgust? All of us are familiar with the splitting headache and varied pains that invariably accompany worry and tension.

None of these effects is imaginary. They are caused by the tightening of muscles and the squeezing of nerves and blood vessels in reaction to emotions. If such a state of mind is prolonged—and with many persons it is continual—it can lead to sickness as serious as any caused by germs.

Doctors warn us that becoming angry or upset can cause the coronary arteries of our heart to squeeze tightly. In time, this can produce a heart attack that is just as fatal as one brought on by physical causes. In fact, the former are much more common than the latter. Likewise, an ulcer resulting from anxiety is just as real and painful as one brought on by wrong diet. These are just two examples of the many hundreds of illnesses which people bring upon themselves by their mental attitudes.

According to Dr. John A. Schindler, author and former Chief Physician of the Monroe Wisconsin Clinic, "The human body is heir to a thousand different ailments and one of them appears to be as common as all other 999 put together. It formerly was known as psychoneurosis. Now it is known as psychosomatic illness. And it is *not* a disease in which the patient merely *thinks* he is sick."

What is the solution to this mounting toll of misery and ill health? The American Medical Association tells us that we must learn to control our thoughts and to think right. It lists eight excellent rules for us to follow:

"1. Quit looking for a knock in your motor. 2. Learn to like your work. 3. Have at least one hobby. 4. Learn to like people. 5. Learn to be satisfied when you can't easily change your situation. 6. Learn to accept adversity. 7. School yourself to learn to say the cheerful, helpful and humorous thing. 8. Learn to face your challenge and your problems with confidence and decision."

This is helpful advice as far as it goes, but it overlooks the most important remedy of all: faith—faith that all will be well, faith that faith will make it so. A vast number of people today are facing life without the buoyant support of this dynamic force. Many of them have a kind of faith, all right, but it is something they keep hidden in a holy niche of their consciousness, taking it out for Sundays and special religious occasions and then putting it carefully away again. They seem to feel that faith belongs solely to the spiritual realm and has no connection with the material world of everyday living. They fail to weave its golden strands into the fabric of their daily life and thus are helpless to handle the constant difficulties they meet.

They worry about their health, finances, homes, jobs, taxes, old age, atomic warfare, the weather, their neighbors. Their minds throng with a thousand flitting images of half-formed worries, doubts and apprehensions. Nothing is too insignificant or farfetched for them to fret about. In fact, a good many persons spend most of their waking hours brooding about something or other. All of this unnecessary tension, this suicidal morbidity, adds up to just one thing: fear—fear of what the future will bring. And this in turn, boils down to the fact that faith is not operating in their lives as it should.

In order for anyone to acquire the faith that will keep him well, it is first necessary for him to realize that it is not a lot of mystical nonsense but is an established scientific fact. It is the heart and core of psychosomatic medicine. It is just as real as electricity.

You do not have to accept it on someone else's say-so; you can experience its truth and effectiveness in your own life any time you desire. Just shove worry and fear to one side and learn to relax. Take each day as it comes and do not fret about tomorrow. This does not mean that you should not plan for the future, but only that you should never worry about it. There is a big difference. Planning is healthy and constructive. It is the positive approach to life. Worry is unhealthy and destructive. It is the negative approach.

If there is the slightest doubt in your mind as to your present thinking habits, it will repay you to examine them carefully and honestly. You may discover that you have been killing yourself on the installment plan. If such be the case, do not worry. Just make up your mind to face the present with courage and the future with optimism and let faith handle the rest.

If you can't go to sleep when counting sheep, here are some other suggestions to help you woo Morpheus.

HOW ABOUT YOUR INSOMNIA?

by JACK MEYER

If someone in your vicinity says, "I slept like a baby last night," do you feel from the bottom of your insomnia like taking a poke at him to erase that well-rested look from his face? Would you also like to have it understood that there is grave doubt in your mind that he is telling the truth?

Perhaps you suspect that you look similar to the bleary-eyed gargoyle you thought you saw leering at your bedroom window in the early-morning fog. What's more, you just can't find a good excuse to kick around and blame your insomnia on. You could kick something else, like the hassock or highboy, but that would be painful and hence defeat your purpose.

Oh sure, you've had insomnia before. You never came right out and gave it a name, because you hoped it wouldn't happen again. Now that it is happening more and more often, you can't avoid giving it its legitimate name.

Since insomniacs aren't an organized lot who elect officers, conduct meetings or engage in campaigns, they can't come to any sweeping conclusions to eliminate their problems. Anyone on his own is bound to be victimized by those resourceful worry-demons that heckle and harass you beyond the point of no return —or so it seems. Once you relax, your guard is down and you have to start coping with your sleeplessness. That is, unless you are just too tired to stay awake at this point—a refreshing alternative that automatically robs you of your insomniac standing.

Sleep is a necessity recognized the world over. The average American goes to bed in the evening. The time of evening varies according to occupation, social habits and whether you watch the late-late TV show. If you are of the rigid-routine rank, you possibly check the thermostat, lock the doors, put out the cat, brush your teeth and do any number of tedium-producing chores before bedding down on your inner-spring. Variations on this theme are many. But whatever the ritual, eventually we all fall into the same class—would-be sleepers.

Here is a familiar picture. Stretched out prone or supine or curled into a crescent, you punch your pillow, bunching it into the right shape or comfortable hollow. A few wriggles and squirms and you're off. That is, you *thought* you were off. That curtain flapping in the window is no dream, and "oh my aching back," how about shifting to the other side of the bed which has fewer rocks in the mattress?

A few adjustments later, you try again. Now you assume more fantastic positions, like the pretzel, the corkscrew, the sheepdog or the Hindu, all of which feel fine for a few minutes. How about that old trick of closing the eyes and grunting like a contented water buffalo?

"We must not take chances on postponing this matter. . . ." Whoops! How did that old speech get in here? Speculations, reviews, previews and just plain worthless niggling ideas keep building up. Problems and doubts are racing around in your fully awakened brain like greyhounds chasing a rabbit around a giant racetrack.

It could, and does, go on indefinitely. You give the pillow another sharp blow. Count sheep—that's it! Uncle Bill used to say that did the trick for him, but then he was a sheep rancher, and counting them must have given him a sense of security. Counting "one, two, three, four" is murderously dull and ought to put anyone to sleep. "One thousand one, one thousand two . . ." counting out loud, much louder than you thought, not only keeps *you* awake but wakes up the rest of the household as well.

When all is quiet and righteous indignation has simmered down, you say to yourself, "Nice try," and scrap sheep counting. Now the thought flashes onto a mystic screen, "Recite poetry." Some rhythmic lines float to the surface, but you can't get enough of them together to make sense. You haven't recited poetry since you were in the eighth grade. You sit up, swaying back and forth in tempo with "Tell me not in mournful numbers, Life is but an empty . . ." an empty *what!* You cudgel your brain and, by that time, sleep seems two million light-years away.

Worry is certainly a sleep robber, especially for those who are fingernail chewers or thumb-twiddlers to boot. If the worries stem from the weight of decisions that must be made in business or personal life, it would be best to face them as squarely as possible or consult a trustworthy person qualified to help you find the answer. One can't wish problems away, but you can lighten them by putting them in their proper perspective.

My doctor set me straight on several facts about insomnia. "It's quite common," he said, deflating me. "Everyone should evolve his own dependable system to resolve the problem." I mumbled something about trying to help, but the doctor seemed lost in thought. In fact, he looked sleepy. "There aren't any snap cures," he yawned.

This all sounds neat and pat in the doctor's office, but I bet him dominoes to dictionaries that it wouldn't last until I got within a foot of my bed that night. After considerable reading, probing and experimenting, I compiled ten points for my friend, the doctor, to sanction. He said, "It looks to me as if the sleeping-pill trade will decline when this gets out."

I hesitate labeling these *rules,* for the connotation has a tendency to rouse us into taking a firm stand to carry them out. This won't woo any sleep.

Assuming, then, that you have a place to sleep and that your rent is paid up, here are some ideas that do not call for undue cunning or wily tricks:

1. Bedtime should not be worry time or planning time for tomorrow. Mental activity of this kind is not conducive to relaxation.

2. Your bed should be comfortable, not too soft or too hard. Used subdued colors in the bedroom and, if possible, do not use the room for other activities such as sewing, desk work or watching TV.

3. Do not be overly concerned or fretful about getting your eight hours of sleep. People vary in their requirements and you may not need that much.

4. Almost everyone has a "getting-ready-for-bed" routine. These preparations, by their very monotony, bring on somnolence. If you must read in bed, better choose something fairly dull so that the drowsy atmosphere created does not dissipate.

5. Don't fret if you don't go to sleep right away. Quiet rest without loss of consciousness is beneficial, too. Shut out noises and light. This is particularly true of unusual sounds such as a dripping faucet, a flapping curtain or thumping blinds.

6. When hunger gnaws, don't resist that snack which will settle the demon. Crackers and milk may sound unexciting, but will fill that hollow which may

have grown to proportions of the Grand Canyon while you were wasting your time fighting it.

7. Smoking and caffeinic drinks, especially if used excessively, may be too stimulating for some. Others, whose systems have adjusted to these stimulants, will snooze away unperturbed.

8. Certain positions are more restful than others. Lying on the side is recommended for adults with a pillow of the right thickness to alleviate shoulder or neck muscle strain. Don't get the idea, however, that if you go to sleep on your side you will wake up in the same position. It can happen, but you may have ended up there after changing positions about forty times during the night.

9. Stretching and yawning help you to let down. Try a nightly "I don't care" attitude. In fact, sprawling and stretching and then reversing the stretch to what I call a "slumping-in-a-heap" feeling makes you feel like drifting off.

10. Your digestion, possible allergies, attitudes and general health play a part in your quest for rest. If you are an insomniac of long standing, losing night after night of sleep, you may not be a subject for self-help. Consult your physician for remedial treatment of possible underlying causes.

You can kid about insomnia just so far, then you've had it. If it is of any help to know that many famous people at one time or another belonged to the ranks of *insomniacs*, cherish the thought. As for me, I'm too slee-eepy!

Tears are the safety valve that could help you add years to your life.

MEN, IT'S OKAY TO CRY!

by RALPH E. PROUTY

One of the most emotion-packed moments in sports history came on July 4, 1939, when the New York Yankees held a "Lou Gehrig Day" at Yankee Stadium. Seldom has there been such a spontaneous outpouring of feeling for an athlete. The recipient of it all, the "Iron Horse," had reached the end of the trail. Actually Gehrig was a dying man, though none of his teammates or fans suspected it.

As the compliments and praises were showered upon him by such dignitaries as Mayor Fiorello LaGuardia and Postmaster General James A. Farley, Lou gulped and fought back the tears. But when Manager Joe McCarthy presented him with a silver trophy from his Yankee teammates, the big athlete broke down and cried.

Other athletes have shed tears in public, and with less provocation. Not many baseball players would cry upon learning that they had been sold to the Yankees. One who did was a Cardinal outfielder, Enos Slaughter. After sixteen years with St. Louis, Slaughter was unexpectedly sold to the Yanks. Enos was so shocked at the idea that the Cards would let him go after such long and faithful service that his only outlet was in tears.

Basketball star Bob Cousy shed a few tears at a celebration in his honor at the Boston Garden. At thirty-four, Cousy was retiring after thirteen years with the Boston Celtics to start a coaching career. The accolade, including a telegram from President John F. Kennedy, was more than the cage star could take. His feeling overflowed through his eyes.

Athletes aren't the only grown men known to cry as an involuntary expression of emotion. Shortly after V-E Day, a colonel in the United States Army was driving through Germany in his small staff car. He passed lines of ragged, tired German soldiers, just released from prison camps, now trudging hundreds of miles back to their homes and families.

"Strange," said the colonel later, "last week I hated their guts. Now I suddenly saw them as human beings hurrying back home to become husbands, rear children and till the soil. Before I realized it, I found that I was crying."

Our culture has taught us for thousands of years that crying is unmanly. Only women weep. Men—especially strong men—suffer in silence. King Lear, Shakespeare's tragic hero, after being dispossessed by his two daughters, suffers the greatest heartbreak of his life. But will he weep? He will not. He says:

> "Let not woman's weapons, water-drops,
> Stain my man's cheeks!"

In other cultures it is quite permissible for a man to shed tears in public. Among the Maoris of New Zealand it is as common and accepted a thing for the warriors to weep as it is for the women. Eskimo men also weep without losing status in the eyes of the community.

It is not uncommon in Latin countries to see men shed tears in public. Perhaps the French, Italians and Spanish are simply more emotional by nature than the rest of us. There is also the possibility that their men realize the value of a good cry now and then.

Scientists have been telling us for the past few years that crying may actually be good for us on occasion. In a recent address to the American Chemical Society, Dr. James O. Bond, distinguished epidemiologist, said that modern man might add years to his life if he would break down and weep once in a while or else find a male equivalent for tears.

"Weeping," said Dr. Bond, "has both a protective and a tonic effect—protective in that it guards the organism against the damaging effects of shock, tonic in that it serves to restore the organism to a state of stability."

When we undergo a severe emotional experience, tension builds up within the body. The body demands some way to release this tension. Crying is nature's way of providing that emotional release. When we refuse to shed tears, the whole body takes the brunt of the emotional discharge. This may upset delicate glandular balances, cause chemical changes in the body, raise hob with your nerves and actually make your body ill.

Noting that American men have been taught that "only sissies cry," Dr. Bond cites the case of the Eskimo man, who is free to weep without the finger of scorn being pointed at him. The doctor notes, at the same time, that psychosomatic disorders are practically unknown among Eskimo men.

Any connection? A good many scientists are beginning to think so. Dr. Walter Alvarez of the Mayo Clinic bears out what Dr. Bond has already said: "Deep emotion that has no vent in tears makes the other organs weep."

Special studies made by the United States Army indicate that men will resort to many reactions before they allow themselves to shed tears. They will grit their teeth, clench their fists, vomit, even faint. But, being red-blooded American boys, they won't cry. That's for softies.

Suppose you saw a picture of a man in public life— a man you respected highly—shedding tears. Would you lose your respect for him? Haven't you yourself ever been in a situation where you felt yourself close to tears?

Stand in front of the faded original of our Declaration of Independence in Washington. Look up at the brooding statue of our Civil War President inside the Lincoln Memorial. Lay your hand on the Liberty Bell in Philadelphia. Walk across Concord Bridge and stand beside the Minute Man. Find yourself blinking to keep the tears back? The associations brought to mind by these objects arouse a flood of emotions that simply demands an outlet. The easiest by far is tears.

Tears aren't always triggered by sorrow, sympathy, grief or a train of thought. Sometimes sheer beauty is enough to bring on an outburst. The late Charles Laughton was once at Chapel Hill to give a program of readings at the University of North Carolina. Walking through the university gardens that afternoon, he came upon a bank of massed daffodils and narcissuses. The sight was so movingly beautiful that Laughton burst into tears.

History records famous men who wept in public. Alexander the Great wept because there were no more worlds for him to conquer. Scipio spoke of "the gracious gift of tears." Abraham Lincoln was proud of his ability to weep for relief and in sympathy, and what Bible reader does not know that Jesus wept.

In our own time, too, outstanding men shed tears in public. Generalissimo Chiang Kai-shek wept at the funeral of one of his generals. General George Patton, after his victory in Europe, wept at a testimonial dinner tendered him in Boston. Even rugged John L. Lewis shed tears as he took his United Mine Workers Union out of the C.I.O.

When TV great Arthur Godfrey fired his star singer, Julius LaRosa, both men shed tears while discussing the affair with reporters. Godfrey wept on another occasion—when he described over coast-to-coast radio the funeral of President Franklin D. Roosevelt. Godfrey was frankly crying as he spoke. No one in America thought less of him.

Only a few years ago, when General Dean was liberated from a North Korean prisoner-of-war camp, he washed away the humiliation and suffering of those years with unrestrained, unashamed tears. Perhaps the greatest humanitarian of our century, Dr. Albert Schweitzer, was known to weep in public.

So next time you feel close to tears, let 'em come. You'll be better off for it. After all, why be a tough guy with a mixed-up inside when it's just as easy to be a little less tough with a well-adjusted inside?

Know what happens when you tie down the saftey valve on a steam engine? The whole thing may blow up. So don't tie down the safety valve on your emotions. Shed a tear if the occasion demands. You may actually be helping yourself live a longer, a happier and a better-adjusted life!

The next time you reach for a cocktail, stop and ask yourself if there isn't a sign before you that reads ...

DANGER! ALCOHOLISM AHEAD

by LILA LENNON

Yes—You *can* become an alcoholic. In fact, if you have already stepped over the thin line that separates the regular social drinker from the *alcohol-dependent* drinker, you may be in danger of taking the next, very short step towards becoming a victim of that incurable disease known as alcoholism.

It can happen to anyone—rich or poor, educated or illiterate, young or old—the more than five million alcoholics in the U.S. come from all levels of society and economic status, from all occupations.

It is estimated that about 71 per cent of the adult population drinks, and that one out of fifteen people will end up as an alcoholic. That one person is, or will become, an alcohol-dependent drinker. Usually, he is not even aware that his drinking has reached this dangerous, pre-alcoholic stage and does not suspect that for him disaster is just around the next corner.

What causes that one person out of fifteen to step into the abyss of excessive, repetitive and uncontrolled drinking? Prevailing scientific opinion is that a combination of physical, psychological and environmental factors are involved, and that alcoholism is in the man—or woman—not in the bottle.

Unfortunately, most people are likely to resent being told they're "drinking too much" and, in addition, they also develop a kind of protective amnesia about how often and how much they drink. Even those who consider themselves just "social drinkers" frequently remain unaware of increased consumption, but the answer is easily obtainable—simply by marking every drink, each day, on a calendar pad for a month. The total may prove to be shocking—and sobering.

For a majority, social drinking creates no problems and does not disrupt their lives in any way; it is the alcohol-dependent drinker who is most likely to acquire the serious, complex disease of alcoholism, and it is a grim fact that 10 per cent of the adult population *are* alcohol-dependent drinkers.

How can you tell how far or how fast you're traveling along the downhill road to alcohol dependency? Your answer to the following questions will help you spot signs that spell *Danger!*

How long have you been drinking?

How much do you drink?

How often?

When?

Why?

Has the amount and frequency of your drinking increased?

Do you feel you cannot have a good time without a drink—that it's a "must" for all social encounters, including golf, fishing, card playing, etc.?

Has the "martini luncheon" become a daily fact of life as a means of selling either your products or services?

Do you anticipate having a drink immediately after work?

Do you make a point of stopping at a bar or heading for the bar car on the train before going home?

Do you have a definite tendency to drink on "signal"—before luncheon, dinner or bedtime to celebrate something or for other "special" reasons? Do you drink every day, for one or more of the following reasons—to erase fatigue, to alleviate boredom, frustration, anxiety or discouragement?

If your answers give you an uneasy feeling that it's time to turn off that downhill road, you can take the following "detours":

Keep an accurate, truthful record of the number of drinks you take.

Never take a drink *every* day.

Don't drink on an empty stomach.

If you feel you "need" a drink—don't take it. Substitute walking, for instance (and for miles, if necessary), for the drink.

Space your drinks. Don't take (or as a guest accept) the second drink for a half hour after you've finished the first. Allow an hour before taking the third, and don't take the fourth.

Dilute the amount of alcohol by sticking to long, weak drinks.

Break the habit of drinking "on signal"—substitute hot strong tea or bouillon before meals, warm cocoa or other caffeine-free beverages before bed.

When you feel especially tired or tense, substitute the hot-tub-soak and cold-shower routine for a drink.

Never, *never* drink in the morning to "overcome" a hangover.

In addition, a frank discussion with your doctor or clergyman, or both, can be helpful in learning how to find other detours that lead away from the road to alcohol dependency.

The alcohol-dependent drinker is already on the

downhill road that can, and will for some, lead to the dead-end street of broken dreams, hopes and lives. But the danger signs are there, if you will slow down, read them . . . and heed them!

Since three minutes of anger will sap your strength quicker than eight hours of work . . .

CAN YOU AFFORD YOUR TEMPER?

by DUANE VALENTRY

Bill Hamilton's job never looked so good as it did the day he walked out the door for the last time. He had one consolation. "Well, I finally told that guy off!"

But this was small comfort. Nor did it stack up well against the necessity of telling the wife she'd have to cut corners until he came up with something.

Bill's temper had cost him another job, his chances of becoming sales manager and his peace of mind. He decided this last blowup had been a lot more expensive than it was worth.

Can you afford your temper? Temper can be the most expensive thing in your life. Ask Bill Hamilton, or the man eating his heart out with remorse in jail because in a fit of rage he broke his crying child's arm. Ask the woman who flares up and loses friends faster than she can make them.

Many unhappy marriages result from the uncontrolled temper of a marriage partner. One man didn't like the way his wife cooked dinner and threw it at her; another raged because his wife spent too much on clothes and ripped everything in her closet.

Childish? Unreasoning? Temper usually is. Even when justified, it's costly to the indulger, according to doctors, psychiatrists and temper-indulgers themselves.

"What I need is to belong to a 'Tempers Anonymous,' an organization like the one drinkers have," says a man with a cocked-trigger temper.

A bad temper is a burden to the one possessing it and to those around him. Like the drinker, he is often a fine person otherwise, intelligent and affectionate, which is why temper has been called the "vice of the virtuous."

Again, like the drinker, he suffers remorse and self-condemnation, often to an agonizing degree. He swears to reform, never to let himself go again and, like the drinker, he doesn't until next time.

The bad-tempered man apologizes for his actions to those he has offended and tries to make up to friends for things he has said and done. Often, because they're friends, they forgive him. But temper has broken many friendships.

Probably more importantly, he can't forgive himself. Each letting-go takes something from him and adds a sickness of soul which is part of the high price of temper. But it is costly to health, too.

"Three minutes of anger will sap your strength quicker than eight hours of work," says the Reverend Charles W. Shedd, who has counseled many burdened with this problem. "Why? Because it has put a terrific strain on your body. When you are angry, your blood rushes to the major muscles of arms and legs. Thus you have greater physical strength, but your brain, lacking its full blood supply, is cut down in efficiency.

This is why you say things you do not mean and do things which seem outlandish."

This is similar to "euphoria," which causes one under the influence of alcohol to do things he will look back on with regret.

Doctors know many of the body's ills come from attitudes of anger, hate and resentment, and that many a sick man or woman recovers by the simple process of substituting patience for impatience, calmness for anger, and love for hate.

Few psychiatrists today tell troubled patients to blow their tops if they feel like it. Such temporary release, they have found, lacks the curative power of replacing hate with love.

"Why keep giving in to a bad habit?" asks Dr. Walter Alvarez, formerly of the Mayo Clinic, in his syndicated medical column. "That only helps it to fasten itself upon you. Fight the habit every day, and eventually you will be free of it, and hence so much nicer a person."

Thousands know the terrible cost of temper to peace of mind. "I'll regret to my dying day the mean things I said to my Dad in an argument—I never had a chance to say I was sorry, he went so quickly," young Fred Nelson commented sadly at his father's funeral.

Anger costs the co-operation and good opinions of others, as well as their affection and regard. Like alcoholism it needs to be faced to be cured.

"We had personnel trouble in our office and lost valuable work time through turnover," relates a once-choleric boss. "Nobody would take my fits of anger very long. I had to get myself in hand—home life has become happier, too."

Temper robs a woman of beauty and a man of dignity. Helen of Troy could not look beautiful in a rage as actress Ava Gardner proved recently when she threw champagne at photographers.

"It is no sin to have a temper, only to go on having it, and prayer has helped many to bring a bad temper under control," recommends the Reverend Charles W. Shedd. "The best way to lose your temper is to lose yourself in God."

Physical action also helps. Breaking something or running around the block works off adrenalin in the system, with no cost involved.

"Every time you get into an argument you have a small chance of boosting your ego and softening the opposition and a big chance of losing a friend and hardening an artery," says Mary Martin, Broadway star, who goes out of her way to avoid a discordant situation.

Self-analysis helps. If temper fits follow a pattern they can be forestalled. Anger may come with fatigue, a let-down or with worry; and half the battle is won if such tendencies are recognized.

John Hudson got in a bad temper at the end of the day when he had to buck traffic and "all those fool drivers." Then he tried calming his thoughts, to think of the other drivers as men like himself, going home. Trying earnestly to "get close to God," before long Hudson was enjoying the trip home and was heard to remark to his wife that traffic had changed a lot. It hadn't; he had.

Henry Drummond's famous essay, "The Greatest Thing in the World," which has helped many overcome tempers, warns that the Bible "again and again returns to condemn it (anger) as one of the most destructive elements in human nature.

"No form of vice, not worldliness, not greed of gold, not drunkenness itself," said Drummond, "does more to un-Christianize society than evil temper. For embittering life; for breaking up communities; for destroying the most sacred relationships; for devastating homes; for withering up men and women; for taking the bloom of childhood; in short, for sheer gratuitous misery-producing power, this influence stands alone."

The price of temper is so high, who can afford it?

———————————————————

You don't have to know how to read a blueprint to learn . . .

HOW TO REBUILD YOUR BODY

by ED SAINSBURY

Would you trade an hour or two a day now for an additional fifteen years of life?

It's not guaranteed, but it's your option to gamble for the privilege, and your chances are better to win than to lose. As horse players say, the odds are right.

A program that can be followed rather easily by any man, and for that matter, by any woman, offers the chance.

Experiments performed over the past twenty years by Dr. Thomas Kirk Cureton of the University of Illinois have pinpointed the path.

Here's the course to greater longevity and more enjoyment of added years, by better health.

1. Walk two miles a day.

2. Perform your own calisthenics before breakfast and before bedtime.

3. Take a cool bath six days a week, a short hot bath on the seventh day, with a brisk rub after each.

4. Play golf or take a long hike, once a week.

5. Eat fewer fried and starchy foods; eat more fruit, vegetables and proteins.

This program was recommended by Dr. Cureton to a fifty-nine-year-old professor who complained of painful feet, high blood pressure, insomnia and excess weight. His recreation had consisted of a little gardening, occasional fishing and some canoeing. He did no regular exercise.

After six months on the recommended program, his over-all fat was reduced 28 per cent; his abdominal fat was decreased 46 per cent; his blood pressure had improved 20 to 41 per cent. His weight had dropped only 2 per cent, indicating that solid tissue had replaced previous flabbiness. His back was 10 per cent stronger, his legs 7 per cent stronger, and his chest expansion was up 4 per cent. Needless to say, his complaints on physical condition largely had vanished.

"The results were obtained by a conscientious individual who worked almost wholly by himself, under guidance," Cureton said. "The results show that an older man can make wonderful progress in reconditioning himself. It is quite possible that this subject also has increased his 'distance from death,' but it is also known that such gains in physical fitness will quickly deteriorate with reversion to sedentary living and overeating."

Tests on one of Dr. Cureton's patients indicated a life expectancy of six years. After six months on the Cureton Cure, his life expectancy, judged by his physical condition, had increased to twenty-one years.

This jump in longevity probably would be greater than the average sedentary businessman could expect, but there's no doubt that if he is in reasonable health when he adopts the program, his life expectancy should improve in some degree during the course.

The physical conditioning is not difficult and a man can continue the program for any number of years.

A physical examination should be a prerequisite for the Cureton course, but if there are no indications of illness, then Dr. Cureton believes there is little chance that the subject will overdo the job. "Most of them quit long before their hearts stop them," he said. A middle-aged office worker might develop sore muscles at first, but as soon as his strengthened heart begins pumping more blood, the soreness should disappear.

Cureton's conclusions were reached after testing thousands of "middle-aged" men—by his classification between the ages of twenty-six and sixty—since he says he detects signs of aging in men at the age of twenty-six. More than five hundred of these subjects went through his course of physical training, and retests at the end of the program showed improved breathing, better heart action, more muscular flexibility, greater strength and more endurance. Cardio-vascular ailments would be negligible among the middle-aged, if they would exercise more, eat less and eat the right foods, he concluded.

Heart trouble and hardening of the arteries, the "spare tire" around the middle, tiredness and feeling old—all are related to the condition of the cardio-vascular system, which is medical jargon for the heart and blood vessels. Cureton has concluded that almost anyone who will take the time and follow a proper conditioning program can do something to improve his cardio-vascular system. But his program is not for reducing, nor for those with physical defects.

Cureton doesn't advocate a quick leap into his program. Instead, he suggests an easy course, gradually working up to the level of the individual's abilities. Nature, he contends, has its own safety check and invariably you will stop yourself well before your heart is even close to giving out. Too little hard work and exercise—not too much—kills off the middle-aged or starts them toward an early grave, he contends.

There can be too much exercise, though. It can be too violent, or you can get too tired when not in condition. If it is too violent, or if the individual isn't quite fit, his progress might be set back three or four days. For the middle-aged, Cureton urges moderate, rhythmic exercise, not competitive, top-speed activity.

Walking or swimming, and exercise, are recommended by Cureton to promote the flow of blood. In rhythmic actions such as walking and swimming, the big muscles in the legs and back push the blood toward the heart, making it stronger, and thus they serve to tone up the entire cardio-vascular system. Large numbers of capillaries close up because of physical inactivity. When the blood gets moving again, in rhythmic exercising, new capillaries open and the blood pressures, both systolic and diastolic, will drop because the ejected blood encounters less resistance and circulates more freely.

Cool baths, or swimming in cold water, are recommended because hot water brings blood to the skin surfaces, which can hold half of the bodily supply, and draws it away from the vital organs, such as the heart, pancreas and liver, where it is needed.

Swimming and walking are among the best conditioners, but climbing, cycling, rowing, horseback riding, dancing, jogging, skating and skiing also are good. You can adopt a different one for each season of the year. Tennis is helpful, but it can be too fast for the unfit. Golf is beneficial because of the necessary walking and sunlight.

Now let's take a look at the Cureton program, as

it applies to you. How can you do it? Or can you do it? It won't be easy, but it can be done.

Arise thirty to forty-five minutes earlier than usual. Take ten minutes for calisthenics, then a cool bath, with a brisk towel rub. Eat a normal breakfast, including fruit, protein and whole grain bread.

Get off the bus, street car or subway, or park your car a mile from the office. Walk the rest of the way briskly. If it's a sunny day, you'll benefit from the ultraviolet rays as well.

Eat a light lunch—a salad perhaps, with whole grain bread. Include proteins. Have a little fruit.

When your work day is done, walk a mile to your car, or before you catch the bus, or to whatever transportation you use. For your evening meal, again whole grain bread, green and yellow vegetables, lean meat, broiled or roasted, or broiled or baked fish for the main course, stewed or fresh fruit for dessert.

Before bedtime, another ten minutes of calisthenics. Or as you progress toward better motor ability, fifteen minutes. It should relax you and prepare you better for a normal night of sleep.

There's no formula for the number of hours of sleep necessary. Most athletes sleep from eight to ten hours a night, Dr. Cureton said. Some sleep more. You sleep according to need, but be sure to get plenty after strenuous exercise.

Your daily routine can be altered, not without some sacrifice perhaps, to comply with other phases of the Cureton Cure. Swim once or twice a week, in a pool in the winter and in warm weather use the available outdoor facilities. Opportunities exist in many areas for golf, dancing, horseback riding, bicycling, skiing or skating. Roller skating is comparable to ice skating. Weekends furnish the time for recreation; you can furnish the motive and probably enjoy it as well.

Benefits continue as long as the conditioning program continues. It prevents fat, and some fat is burned away. Digestion improves. The mind is clearer. The individual has more pep and feels younger, because his body actually is physiologically younger and in better condition.

You probably can't "find" time for exercise. In this respect the office worker rarely progresses out of the realm of wishful thinking. But with the *planned* fitness program you can delay the onset of old age's physical and psychological problems for ten to fifteen years.

The thorns in the Cureton Cure, for many office workers, would be these: Cut out the use of alcohol and tobacco. Or at least cut down on them. Tests indicate that smoking reduces the endurance of young men, he said, and nonsmokers improve more rapidly in his tests. He has not run controlled studies on the effect of smoking on middle-aged men, but he urges them to quit, if possible, or at least cut down.

Dr. Cureton himself is a testimonial to the value of his system. At the age of forty-two, on a dare, he ran the training obstacle course of the Air Force at Chanute Field, Rantoul, Illinois, and broke the course record by eight seconds. Cureton follows his own advice. His favorite exercise is swimming. He averages about half a mile a day in the water, swimming usually from noon until one o'clock. Most days he swims thirty laps without pause in the University of Illinois pool, using the breast, back and crawl strokes. Three or four times a week, in good weather, he runs three to four miles a day. He wants to stay fit himself, and he does, amazing his audiences with demonstrations of his physical skill. But he feels that he does nothing remarkable, only what anyone keeping fit can do.

Cureton, who has run his tests on Olympic athletes from many nations, has discovered that wheat germ oil has been beneficial in improving athletic abilities. But this doesn't mean that you, by taking wheat germ oil, can find the easy cure to body welfare.

In 1953-54, Cureton ran tests on two groups of men, using fresh wheat germ oil with one group and another oil (of equal energy value) with the other. The group which took exercise and neutral oil showed a 19 per cent increase in endurance running time on a treadmill. The following year, with wheat germ oil and exercise, the increase was 25 per cent, despite the higher level of performance at the starting point.

The second group, which had exercise and wheat germ oil in the first year, increased 51.5 per cent. But the following year, on exercise with neutral oil, the group showed a 5.6 per cent decrease in treadmill endurance.

Cureton also cites the performances of two University of Illinois athletes, hurdler Willard Thomson and swimmer Jody Alderson, as examples of the value of wheat germ oil in physical endurance. Thomson, after a slump, thought he had gone stale, but after three weeks of wheat germ oil, he began to improve. In a month he equalled his best time; in six weeks he broke his best previous time. In eight weeks he won the national championship.

Miss Alderson, Cureton said, showed "almost miraculous results." She never had won a championship, but under seventy-five yards she was the equal in speed of anyone in the nation. Beyond that distance, her endurance was poor. After six weeks of wheat germ oil, she began to improve. In eight more weeks she broke her own previous marks, and went on to win both the national indoor and outdoor championships, setting a national record.

Cureton knows what makes athletes perform at new peak levels. He has examined and worked with and advised Gil Dodd, John Marshall, Roger Bannister, Ezzard Charles and others. Their bodies may be better developed or in better condition than your own. But they work the same way.

The Cureton Cure, a sane and consistent program of easy exercise and more intelligent diet, has worked for thousands. It can work for you.

Come on, men, do you want to live forever?

8 OPPORTUNITY UNLIMITED

A wise man will make more
opportunities than he finds.
                    —*Francis Bacon*

He was a pioneer in his field and his writings became . . .

A MIRACLE OF
POSITIVE THINKING

by WILLIAM L. ROPER

"Since 1892, I've had nothing to do, do . . . do . . . do . . ."

While thousands of idle discouraged Americans chanted this ditty of defeatism during the devastating panic of 1893-98—a time of riots, hunger marches and threats of revolution—one American was busy working on a "success" book that was to bring new hope to millions and play an important role in restoring prosperity to America.

His name was Orison Swett Marden. The book, the first of more than forty he devoted to the theme of winning personal success by positive thinking and self-discipline, was *Pushing to the Front.*

Early in life, Marden, an orphan at seven, had read Dr. Samuel Smiles's book *Self-Help,* and decided there must be a formula for achievement. Later, in seeking the reasons why some men achieve greatness and wealth despite all kinds of obstacles, he interviewed Thomas A. Edison, John D. Rockefeller, Andrew Carnegie, Alexander Graham Bell and other successful men.

Marden's research convinced him that there were certain basic rules for accomplishment: self-confidence: positive, creative thinking; hard work; concentrated effort; singleness of purpose and clean living. Other men before Marden had discovered these virtues, but he was one of the first to formulate them into a pattern for successful living.

Today the value of these rules for mental discipline is widely recognized. And they are just as useful now as they were then. By applying them, young persons today have a definite advantage over those who think one must have a barrel of luck or a magic pull to win.

Marden's own life demonstrated the truth of his success philosophy.

One night in 1892, just as the great Depression was getting under way, Marden's Midway Hotel in Kearney, Nebraska, burned to the ground. With it was burned the manuscript of his "success" book, *Pushing to the Front.*

The loss was a severe blow to his dwindling fortune, acquired by careful saving and prudent investment. But what grieved him far more was the destruction of his manuscript.

What would he do now? Even before the embers stopped smoking, Marden made up his mind.

Renting a barren room over a livery stable, Marden started to work, rewriting his book. That winter he lived on $1.50 a week. He was sustained by his enormous self-confidence and faith in his idea, although the clouds of the coming Depression grew darker.

For years he had studied and analyzed the techniques used by so-called self-made men in attaining success. He was convinced others could use the same methods effectively. That was the purpose of his book —to show young men and women how to make their dreams come true. Its theme, stated simply, was: "He can who thinks he can."

Marden was deeply in debt when spring came. Manfully, he struggled to complete the book. Meanwhile, the soup lines in the big cities grew longer, and panic mounted.

When Marden offered his "success" book to publishers, they rejected it. Some countered: "How can people buy books when they can't buy bread?"

Marden realized now that all of the rules he had formulated for overcoming obstacles and achieving success were faced with a decisive test. One of the chapters in his book was about "Grit" and the courage to carry on despite difficulties. Marden had those qualities.

He recalled Mirabeau's classic phrase: "Nothing is impossible to the man who can will."

And Marden himself had written: "The strong-willed, intelligent, persistent man will find or make a way where, in the nature of things, a way can be found or made."

So packing a suitcase with his few possessions, including the manuscript of his precious book, he left Kearney for Chicago in 1893.

There he found temporary employment as manager of the Park Gate Hotel during the World's Columbian Exposition. When off duty, he visited local publishers, trying to persuade one to publish his book. None would risk it.

A few days after the Fair closed, Marden journeyed to Boston where he had friends. It was there he had received his B.A. degree from Boston University in 1877 and an M.D. from Harvard in 1882.

But business conditions in Boston weren't much better than in Chicago. That was the spring that Jacob S. Coxey led his army of twenty thousand unemployed, half-starved men in a march on Washington. Pessimism reigned. America was in the doldrums. Businessmen hesitated to try new ventures. Hoarding was common.

How could America be saved and business rejuvenated? A few political leaders advocated a foreign war. Others proposed doles.

Then, in 1894, a miracle happened. Marden, with the aid of friends who were impressed by the merit of his idea and his own unshaken faith in it, got his book published. The first edition of *Pushing to the Front* sold out quickly. A second went equally fast. In spite of hard times, people were finding money to buy the book.

For panic-sick America, the volume's courageous, optimistic philosophy was just what the doctor ordered. It gave the discouraged new hope, new faith in themselves. Undoubtedly, it helped to change the mental outlook of thousands, and so became a turning point in the nation's economy.

Eventually, the book went through 250 editions and was translated into many foreign languages. In Japan and several other foreign countries, it was used extensively in the public schools. Queen Victoria wrote a letter commending it.

Marden followed *Pushing to the Front* with other books based on the same general theme: *Rising in the World* (1896), *Every Man a King* (1906), *The Optimistic Life* (1907), *He Can Who Thinks He Can* (1908), *Everybody Ahead* (1917), *Ambition and Success* (1919) and *Masterful Personality* (1921). In 1911, he brought out a new and enlarged edition of *Pushing to the Front*. It continued to be a best seller.

Thirty of his books were translated into German and more than three million of them were sold in twenty-five languages.

There is an inspiration in Marden's life as well as in the books he wrote. Born near Thornton, New Hampshire, in 1850, he became self-supporting at an early age. While attending Boston University and later at Harvard, he waited on tables and developed a catering business to pay his way. He had saved nearly $20,000 before completing college. With this nest egg, he bought an old tourist hotel on Block Island, off Newport, Rhode Island, and by intelligent promotion developed his holdings until he owned controlling interests in five hotels, including the Midland in Kearney. With the Depression, his hotel business collapsed and he was near bankruptcy when the Midland burned that night in 1892.

In addition to writing books, Marden was publishing a successful national magazine when he died on March 10, 1924.

By his own yardstick, he was a success. In *Rising in the World*, he had written: "The greatest thing a man can do in this world is to make the most possible out of the stuff that has been given him. This is success, and there is no other."

Marden made the most of what he had, using one theme as the basis for forty books. And in a period of tight money, his first book had become a best seller. Even more importantly he helped to inspire a nation at a time when the gospel of positive, courageous thinking was desperately needed.

GET OFF THE TREADMILL!

by W. CLEMENT STONE

Centuries ago in China there was a great drought. Rice then, as it is now, was the staple food of the Chinese. It was also a medium of exchange. It was money. The rice fields were dying with thirst. Without rain to water them, there would be famine, sickness, even death for the people!

A young farmer whose name has long been forgotten was sitting on a river bank. This young man was the father of three children—all with beautiful brown eyes. He was the husband of a woman who shared all he had, including labor in the field. He had just returned from the village shrine where he had prayed for hours —for rain.

As he sat on the ledge looking at the water of the winding river, the stories told to him by his grandfather kept bothering him—stories of the great drought of another generation. Hundreds of thousands of people died because of famine. This young man wanted his wife and children to live. He, too, wanted to live.

What could he do? With the flash of inspiration that comes from a burning desire—or could it have been an answer to his prayers?—he had a vision.

This young Chinese had a treadmill that was propelled by an ox. When the animal walked, he was forced to move in a circle as the outside of the wheel turned. In his mind's eye, the farmer pictured two large wheels supported by an axle in a horizontal position. Boards were firmly attached as steps between these two wheels. A series of buckets hung on the outside of one wheel. These buckets would scoop up water from the river as the treadmill, in turning, rose from its lowest point. They would dump the water into a trough that would carry it to the rice field as the wheel revolved downward from its highest position.

He was unable to visualize his ox treading such a contraption. "I would do the work of an ox to save my family," he thought. Then he got into action! He called together a group of farmers, all of whom were faced with the same problem. He explained his plan. Together they made treadmills that brought the water from the river to the rice fields above. Since that time, there hasn't been a famine because of lack of rain.

Centuries ago, the treadmill was an invention of great benefit. But what about today? Men or women in many parts of the world are still doing the work of an animal on the same type of treadmill invented by a young Chinese farmer who was a benefactor to his people. Hour after hour—day after day—step by step—they tread.

To the traveler, this sight is interesting, strange and picturesque. Yet in this modern machine age, such wearisome, endless toil seems needless.

Perhaps you are on a treadmill—not one that raises water from a river to the rice fields above, but one just as wearisome, just as needless and far more frustrating. You might say to the wife of the Chinese farmer: "Get off the treadmill!" Yet in his wisdom, the Chinese farmer might respond: "Why don't you get off your treadmill?" Perhaps you and the Chinese farmer would find it just as easy or just as hard. Why? You would need to take time to stop and think. You may need to develop self-motivation. You may need

to develop a burning desire. With these, you could
find the way.

Just like the young Chinese farmer whose name has
long been forgotten, you too can . . . *get off the treadmill!*

---

*Miracles begin to happen when you change
your* I Can't *philosophy to* I Can.

A HOME FOR TEN CENTS

by BEN SWEETLAND

John Doyce was forty-five years old. He was a house
painter, married, the father of two children. He was
working in my living room when he paused, turned to
me and said, "You don't know how lucky you are.
I'd give anything to have a home of my own."

"Why don't you?" I asked.

John looked at me with an expression which clearly
indicated his surprise that I should ask such a seemingly nonsensical question. Laying his brush down and
leaning against his ladder, he spent fully five minutes
telling me why he did not own a home. I was reminded of the cost of bringing up two children; how
hard youngsters are on their clothes; the inevitability
of bills for the doctor and medicine; the high and
rising cost of living. He considered himself lucky and
a good manager to come out even at the end of the
month, let alone purchase a home.

Having felt I was properly put in my place, John

picked up his brush and continued the rhythmic swing right and left as he brought freshness to the walls.

While my painter friend continued his occupation of surface transformation, I picked up an empty candy box and, with the aid of adhesive tape, bound the cover so that it could not be removed and with my pocket knife carved a neat slot in the top of the box, giving it the appearance of a small savings bank. Then, with my ball-point pen, I lettered neatly on the side of the box: "Building Fund."

Noon arrived, and after John Doyce had squatted on the floor with his lunch box between his legs, I approached him with a question quite provocative. "Let me have a coin—any coin," I commanded. Reaching down in his pocket he produced an array of small change, pennies, a nickel or two, a dime, etc. I reached over, picked up a ten-cent piece from his hand and dropped it through the slot in my improvised bank.

Almost with the ceremony of laying a cornerstone, I presented the box to the puzzled painter with the statement: "John, with this important step you have just taken, the home of your dreams is now on its way."

I didn't give him a chance for questioning, but for several minutes I held the floor with a flow of logic he could not dispute.

Saving is a habit—just as spending is a habit. The one who acquires a habit of saving will find it just as easy to adjust his expenditures so that a portion of every paycheck is saved, as the opposite type will find it seemingly necessary to spend every penny received.

John was told that every time he got any money at all, he was to take some of it, if only the tiniest portion, and put it in the box. He did admit that he could do this, but his attitude expressed his doubt that such dribbles would ever amount to anything of importance, especially a sum which could figure in the purchase of a house.

It would have been appropriate to revert to the timeworn illustration, "Mighty oaks from little acorns grow." But I am sure John, with his quizzical mind, would have told me that he would not want to wait the length of time normally required to convert an acorn into a mighty oak.

Houses are built by placing brick upon brick or board upon board. They do not come into being instantly, as if through the wave of a magic wand. The completed structure represents a myriad of small operations. As in travel, regardless of the distance, it it must be covered mile by mile.

In my busy life, counselling with people constantly, both personally and via television and radio, it is simple and quite natural to lose touch with individual cases. This was true so far as John Doyce was concerned. He had slipped my mind completely—until the mailman handed me a neatly printed invitation to a house-warming—and, to my pleased amazement, it was for the new home of Mr. and Mrs. John Doyce.

It was a charming home, quite modern. The large living room had its dining area adjacent to a glamorous kitchen which would arouse the envy of most housewives. There was a master bedroom and two of the most interesting rooms for the children. The center of activity for the house-warming was in the rumpus room—or what is now frequently referred to as the social hall.

It was a long time before I gained the opportunity of congratulating this proud home owner. He and his happy wife were busily engaged in conducting tours of inspection through the newly acquired domicile.

Finally, literally grabbing John by the arm, I sat him down at a table on the terrace, and I relaxed as he unfolded a story which proved highly inspirational, even though it was based on fundamentals I knew so well.

The most interesting part of John's story was not what you might expect, how pennies grow into dollars, dollars into tens, tens into hundreds and hundreds into thousands.

"My greatest victory," exclaimed Doyce thoughtfully, "was learning that *I Can* instead of *I Can't*."

He continued, "Up to the time I worked in your home, I was definitely certain a home was for the other fellow, not for me. Living from pay-day to payday without having a cent saved, your query as to why I didn't own a home came as a paradox. We are not extravagant. We had always felt we lived modestly so that to save for a home, as I thought at that time, would have meant a sacrifice too great to impose upon my family."

Determination to accomplish does not always imply sacrifice. It calls into play one's resourcefulness to augment his present income—thereby enabling him to reach his objective. As this painter saw his spare change growing into bankbook figures, his enthusiasm mounted to such an extent that he sought overtime work. And since he had been able to live and save on his regular income, he wisely took the entire proceeds of his extra work and added it to his now established building fund. Of course, such a move on his part caused his savings curve to ascend abruptly.

The head of a family recently told me that the very high price of steaks and meat in general caused him to live on less money. The family budget, being too small to permit the luxury of fillets and prime roasts, forced his wife to call upon her ingenuity in preparing tasty dishes from less expensive items of food. Stews, with an abundance of nourishing vegetables, were often found on the menu. The less expensive fowl supplied many tasty, satisfying meals. Instead of too frequent pots of dollar-a-pound coffee, the family found it was helping the nervous system by using less of the enchanting beverage.

The Doyce family followed this sound pattern in meal planning, which added more speed to the mounting building fund. And as the rejoicing husband told me, they were actually living better than they had been before. This is understandable when we realize that merely tossing a steak into the broiler takes much less mental effort than planning a meal requiring combinations of many ingredients.

Since this objective has been attained, will the Doyce family revert to their former living patterns? No sir-e-e! Buying this home is merely the beginning. They have started another building fund—this one to enable them to acquire a piece of income property, a house of two or more rentable flats. "And that is not all," he added almost boastfully. "After I get my income property, I'm going into the painting contracting business for myself and have others working for me, instead of being dependent on others for a job."

"What's this?" I asked as I was preparing to leave the memorable housewarming. I was looking at an interesting plaque built into a niche in the entrance hall. Inlaid in a polished piece of walnut burl was a dime and around it were engraved the words: "The Foundation on Which This Home Was Built."

My thoughts went back to the workman painting the walls in my home who so solemnly said: "I'd give anything to own a home of my own."

When was the last time you tried to punch a hole in the sky?

MAKE THE IMPOSSIBLE YOUR GOAL!

by DR. HAROLD BLAKE WALKER

Test pilots, punching into the stratosphere, climbing to undreamed heights in jet and rocket planes, have a phrase they use to describe their work.

They call it "punching holes in the sky."

That is what we were meant to do with our lives, to climb beyond humdrum, reach up beyond preoccupation with gadgets and things, press on beyond "the little aims that end with self."

We aim too low. When it comes to living, we are masters of the mediocre, satisfied with good enough. After all, we are human, we tell ourselves. We are reasonably respectable, by the world's standards. Maybe we are a bit selfish and more than a little stubborn, but so is everybody else we know. Maybe we have prejudices and jaundiced opinions, but who doesn't?

The ideals of the Divine adventure seem quite impossible. The sky is too high to think of punching holes in it. It is the impossible that stops us. But nonetheless it is the challenge of the impossible that gets life out of its rut and onto a highway that goes somewhere. It makes life interesting and thoroughly worth living.

So a weary, weatherbeaten collection of acrobats learned when their act was falling flat. Bosley Crowther describes how they tried to coax a little laughter and applause from a vaudeville audience with their stale routine. Then one of them came down to the footlights and, in a voice that betrayed grim despair, announced to the audience: "We will now do a trick that's impossible."

Thereupon his fellows leaped to frightening perches, the audience woke up, the top man clapped his hands with bristling confidence . . . and out went the lights. When the lights came on, the smiling acrobats were posing proudly in the center of the ring, the impossible quite obviously accomplished. The audience gave them a big hand.

The lights did not go out in the first century when a strange collection of men and women challenged the shoddy standards of the Roman Empire in the name of an "impossible" dream called Christianity. Strange, too, how humanity woke up when they got busy "punching holes in the sky" and began to upset the world.

To be sure, Rome was not built in a day, and life becomes neither a spiritual success nor a moral failure overnight. Thomas a Kempis had it right when he wrote: "If every year we would root out one vice, we would soon become perfect."

That may be overoptimistic, but at least there is a kernel of truth in it. And when you get at the business of punching holes in your little two-by-four sky, anything can happen. The Wright brothers managed to fly a hundred feet off the ground, and that seemed like a miracle. Then we thought the sky really had been pierced when we got to five thousand feet. Now we crash through sixty thousand feet and know we have by no means reached the limit.

Start with yourself as you are and root out the worst in yourself. Maybe you have a long way to climb, but you have to start somewhere. Possibly you have a stubborn streak that makes you a problem at home, in the office or even in your club. Start there and see what God can do with your stubbornness. Get Him into your thinking when you are standing sternly for your own way and making everybody miserable.

Don't be disappointed if you can't overhaul yourself from top to bottom overnight. There is more than a hint of warning in the comment of an illiterate farmer intent on learning to read and write. After some study, he took his pencil and began scribbling. Suddenly he shouted to his wife: "Maria, come here. I can write." She looked at his doodling and said: "Wonderful. What does it say?" "One thing at a time," he said, "I haven't learned how to read yet."

Start where you are, with the things in you that sometimes make you hate yourself. Take one thing at a time, and put God's strength beside your own weakness. The only true failure lies in failure to start.

At the very least, you can be better than you are if you have the wit to reach beyond your grasp and faith enough to believe you can be what you ought to be.

Whatever your age may be it's not too late for your . . .

ASSIGNMENT: SUCCESS

by M. LINCOLN SCHUSTER

Exactly fifty years ago, I learned for the first time . . . and I learned it the hard way, as a member of a graduating class which was of course a captive audience, that the traditional commencement day address is far too long, too vague, too soporific. I resolved then and there to do all I possibly could to correct this situation. For five decades, I have waited patiently for an opportunity to do so, and now, thanks to the editorial hospitality of *Success Unlimited,* I am privileged to *actively transmit,* rather than to *passively receive,* such baccalaureate advice and counsel.

In that spirit, I have, therefore, drawn on the Wisdom of the Ages and the wit of my contemporaries for a few short sentences based on long experience— all of them guaranteed to be brief, specific and designed entirely for their instant applicability, so that each and every senior or graduate can say: *"This means me!"*

First, begin at once (not today or tomorrow or at some remote indefinite date, but right now, at this precise moment) to choose *some subject, some concept, some great name* or *idea* or *event in history on which you can eventually make yourself the world's supreme expert.* Start a crash program immediately to qualify yourself for this *self-assignment* through the three R's of modern adult education—*reading, research* and *reflection!*

I don't mean the sort of expert who avoids all the small errors as he sweeps on to the grand fallacy, but rather one who has *the most knowledge, the deepest insight and the most audacious willingness to break new ground by defining his terms and actually examining all the alternatives and consequences.*

Such a disciplined form of *self-education* will unify your studies in the years ahead, both in college and after college, will give you prestige, eminence and world-wide contacts through your correspondence and fellowship with other people interested in the same specialty. It will add *a new dimension* and *a new unity* to your entire education, and will give you a passionate *sense of purpose,* a *postgraduate objective for your growth and your life work.*

Thus, in the deepest and best sense, you will make friends and influence people, *especially yourself.* The cross-fertilization of ideas will become an exciting and unending adventure that will add a new total perspective to your entire life—just as a God-intoxicated man like Spinoza specialized on rainbows and through that extracurricular program mastered the trade of lens grinding, while creating new concepts in physics, in optics and in the structure, speed and measurement of light.

Second, master the art and technique not merely of rapid reading but *creative* reading and *creative* research. Learn how to use a library and how to build a home library of your own. Back in 1913, high school graduates were still singing the old refrain: *"No more pencils, no more books, no more teacher's saucy looks."* They were throwing away their books and saving their diplomas. I say, *do just the opposite.* Forget your diploma, or throw it away, but *save your books* and *use them night and day.*

Third, learn the supreme art of getting sixty seconds out of a minute, sixty minutes out of an hour, twenty-four hours out of a day. You have as much time as anyone else your age. *Save it, hoard it, plug up all the leaks.* If necessary, stand on the street corner, cap in hand like a mendicant, and beg all the passers-by for the seconds and minutes and hours and days they waste.

Fourth, master the basic art of preparation: Discipline yourself to do your homework first, especially after you finish your formal education. Remember, always, in the words of Pascal, that *chance (or fortune) favors the prepared mind.*

Fifth, begin *now* and learn the art and science of

preventive medicine. Prepare to outperform and outlive your doctors. Emerson said it best: *"Give me health and a day, and I will make the pomp of emperors ridiculous."*

Sixth, work hard, think big, and always have a *dream.* And, above all, concentrate on implementing that dream, beginning with a detailed blueprint and plan for your agenda, your priorities, your *first things first.* Put a firm foundation under your castles in Spain; in the form of these step-by-step, play-by-play specifics that make your dream come true.

Seventh, remember the three challenging questions of the great Hebraic sage Hillel: "If you don't care for yourself, *who will?* If you care *only* for yourself, who are you? If not now, *when?"*

Eighth, remember the words of H. L. Mencken that most people don't recognize opportunity when it comes along, because usually it is disguised as hard work.

Ninth, always keep in mind the maxim of my first and foremost editor, Herbert Bayard Swope of Joseph Pulitzer's old New York *World,* who said: "I can't give you *any* formula for *success,* but I can give you a sure formula for failure—*try to please everybody."*

Tenth, remember with Robert Ingersoll that the time to be happy is *now;* the place to be happy is *here; the way to be happy is to make others so.*

9   SALES
UNLIMITED

*Sales are contingent upon the attitude
of the salesman—not the attitude of
the prospect.*
—*W. Clement Stone*

It's great to be a president of a corporation (or an executive in a responsible position) . . . if you can take it. Perhaps you can. Perhaps you can't. But this article may help you crystallize your thinking about yourself. It may motivate you to higher achievement or give you ideas for a healthier, happier mental attitude toward your present work, your present position and the jobs you might like to hold in the future. For many of the principles are applicable to all those who hope to be, or are, in a position of leadership.

REMINISCING . . .
FROM NEWSBOY TO PRESIDENT

by W. CLEMENT STONE

At the age of six I sold newspapers at 31st and Cottage Grove in the city of Chicago. Today I am president of Combined Insurance Company of America, each of its subsidiaries and several other organizations. And there is a relationship between the newsboy and the president: experience, know-how and sales activity knowledge.

The saying "a salesman is born . . . not made" is a fallacy, as any successful sales manager should know. And it is also true: a successful president or executive, teacher, lawyer, doctor, inventor, scientist, philosopher, artist or genius is not born . . . he, too, is made. Self-made. And each is measured by the results he obtains . . . his achievements.

For every *normal* person is endowed with great mental capacities. Few use and develop their natural abilities sufficiently to reach the many goals they could achieve. And this applies to all of us. But we can develop our abilities more fully in the future if we are motivated to pay the price. We can begin right now . . . to develop the *want-to* (self-motivation), learn the *know-how* (experience) and acquire the necessary *activity knowledge*.

The price? Regular investment in *study, thinking and planning time,* followed through with action . . . *work*. But with proper motivation, know-how, activity knowledge and achievement, work becomes fun. This I learned from experience.

As a newsboy I learned a lot that helped me later as a salesman, sales manager and executive, even though I didn't realize it at the time. I know now that I began to learn then that if I couldn't solve a problem one way, I could another. Thus that first day when I tried to sell papers at 31st and Cottage Grove, a then busy business intersection, the newsboys who were older and bigger than I beat me up to keep me from interfering with their sales. That's why I walked into Hoelle's Restaurant and completely sold out my stock of papers. This eventually led me to realize that every disadvantage can be turned to an advantage if one tries to solve his problem.

Also as a newsboy I began to learn how to overcome fear . . . through action; the value of persistence when it made sales; and how to sell by using a method others were afraid to use: cold-canvassing, that is, calling on business people in business places without an introduction. That's the way I sold insurance. And that's the reason I sold as many accident policies in a single week as many insurance men sell over a period of many months. Why?

As a newsboy I was motivated by necessity. I had borrowed the money to buy the papers. I had to sell them to repay the loan and make a profit. Also as a salesman, a sales manager and an executive, necessity has become a wholesome motivating factor in the solution of problems. Many of the principles I learned selling newspapers between the ages of six and thirteen I have been able to apply in my business activities in adult life. Here are a few examples, followed by statements of the principles involved.

The success in selling newspapers in Hoelle's Restaurant on the first day was repeated day after day. Also, in developing a system for the sale of accident and health insurance, I did that which most insurance men didn't do: at the time of the renewal of a policy I did not merely send a notice but I personally called on each client to renew. Thus I guaranteed the renewal, sold additional protection when needed by my client and increased my number of customers in his place of business.

> *Determine the principles which bring success and those which bring failure. Employ the principles that bring success, and avoid those which bring failure.*

At the age of twelve I entered a hospital to try to sell my papers by calling room to room. I reasoned that the patients would make good prospects and I could see a lot of persons in a short space of time. Because I sold more papers per hour of effort through this experience than any other, I repeated it daily. And in later years, as an insurance salesman, I used exactly the same principle in selling to employees, during business hours, in the largest banks, department stores, government buildings, railway offices, hospitals and other institutions in the United States.

Relate, assimilate and use principles that are successful in one activity . . . in related activities.

Sell in large institutions where . . . others are afraid to sell.

Make greater profits in less selling time by concentrating your efforts in an area where there are a large number of prospects, and thus eliminate waste in travel time.

Go where the money is.

Where there is nothing to lose by trying, and a great deal to gain if successful, by all means try.

And I learned something else by selling newspapers in the hospital. When I started I thought the patients would be there for several days, so I began to make collections once a week. But I soon found that many of my patients didn't stay an entire week. So I collected daily. Also my profits increased because of daily gratuities rather than weekly. Perhaps collecting for the newspapers at the time of delivery is one of the reasons why I later, in selling insurance, made it a practice to collect the premium at the time of application.

Get your money at the time of sale.

At the age of seven or eight, I liked movies, and I probably saw more movies than any youngster I have ever known. There was a large movie house at 31st and Prairie near the apartment where we lived, and a smaller one five blocks west of us. At the larger theater the management, to get business, gave each paying customer a white ticket. The white ticket gave admission to the balcony seats for the following evening. So I would wait outside the theater for the white ticket someone might not want.

Now the smaller theater competed by allowing children free if accompanied by their parents. I went in as a child of couples of all ages. As I look back,

I think the owner knew, for he never said anything and didn't allow any of his employees to stop the practice.

As a salesman selling in large establishments, I obtained permission to sell from the owner by asking him for permission. He had nothing to lose; his employees and I had a lot to gain.

If a person has nothing to lose by giving, and you have lots to gain by asking, give him the opportunity to grant you the favor that costs him nothing.

Now of course, I didn't understand these principles as a newsboy. And as a salesman while I was searching to develop a success formula, I didn't realize that I was using many of the same principles I had employed in my first business venture, selling newspapers. Even when I established my own insurance agency at the age of twenty, and later trained salesmen to use those techniques I had found successful in my personal selling, I wasn't aware of the relationship. The discovery of the connection between the principles used in my early experiences and those I subsequently had, became crystal clear when I worked on the manuscript for my book, *The Success System That Never Fails.*

"President" is defined as the chief officer of a corporation, society or the like. A man in business for himself has the same responsibility as the president of a corporation.

In a sense a foreman, department head, superintendent, sales manager or officer of a company has many of the responsibilities of a president or the owner of a business, even though the area of responsibility is smaller. As an individual, to be successful he must employ the same basic principles that are necessary for success in the job he has; also in preparation for the promotion he would like to achieve.

And this is true of a salesman, office employee or laborer.

For every individual must start with himself. He must be self-made. Therefore it is desirable to motivate ourselves to higher achievement and continually to search for ideas that will bring about a healthier, happier mental attitude towards our present work, our present position and those positions we might like to hold in the future. The basic principles are applicable to everyone. And in the end our success will be evaluated by results—our achievements.

If you call yourself a salesman perhaps you'll change your mind in the next few minutes.

SO YOU'RE A SALESMAN

by BOB GRINDE

I'm going to do something right now that I've wanted to do for a long, long time. I'm going to give you the truth in massive doses today. I'm going to strip off all the fluff, all the candied little phrases that have been tossed at us salesmen over the years. I'm going to get down to the bare facts about nine out of ten so-called salesmen.

I'm going to get so honest with you today, Brother, that you're going to squirm. I'm going to crack open that protective shell you've been hiding behind for years and talk to the inner you.

First, before I let go with the big guns, let me qualify my message. This message is not directed at the one salesman in ten who is helping produce about ninety per cent of the business. This message is directed to the other nine who have found such a goldmine in selling that they've been able to make a sort of living all these years without ever really trying.

So you're a salesman. Brother, when you tell me that, prove it. There is only one real test to go by: how much can you produce? What have you produced?

How much? That's just what I thought. You see when you take a good straight look at yourself, you find that the excuses you've been feeding your wife for years and the alibis you've been giving your sales manager, time after time, don't look so pretty. Oh, sure, you've been able to make a sort of living but if you're a salesman, why aren't you well off financially? I'll tell you why. It's because you haven't earned the right to be rich and that's the flat-out truth, Brother.

In my office I have a little old sign that I picked up years ago that has a picture of a tramp on it. The tramp is saying, "I'd give a thousand dollars to be one of them millionaires." Now that message is worth just a smile or two until you get down and explore the hidden truth behind it. Hundreds of thousands of salesmen are in the same boat with that tramp. They'd give a thousand dollars' worth of effort and wish for a million dollars in results. They've never made an all-out effort to really turn on the heat and sell. They're so used to just getting by that they've never really gotten a picture of what it means to go first class.

So you're a salesman? Brother, when you tell me that, prove it. What sort of clothes do you wear? Do you think you can reflect prosperity walking around in a bargain basement suit? Did you ever put on a real quality hat and try going first class? Did you ever buy the best tie in the store and notice the difference in the way it ties, looks and feels? Did you ever put on a fine quality coat and notice how the quality and quantity of your orders will go up immediately?

Ah, you say, I can't afford that. Well, of course you can't if you're not a salesman but, Brother, once you get a picture of the real riches all around you in this business of selling, why you can't afford to go any other way but first class. It's out there for you. All you've got to do is earn it. So you're a salesman? Brother, when you tell me that, prove it.

Squirm, Brother, squirm. I'm going to ask you the big one now. How are you treating your family? Can they look up to you as a real success or are you going along year after year, feeding this goulash of excuses about how business is tough, how you almost closed this sale, how you almost did that. Aren't you tired of kidding yourself and others? Wouldn't it be a lot easier, right now, to make a decision to go out and earn the right to bigger things? Men who have earned the right to call themselves salesmen don't bring home excuses; they bring home the bacon. So you're a salesman? Brother, when you tell me that, prove it.

I know what it is to fluff off time. I know what it is to go to a movie instead of making that next call. I know what it is to watch a ball game instead of watching for the prospect's signature on the dotted line. I know what it is to lie to yourself because I've done it. You see, they say it takes one to know one. I know what it is to make a couple of half-hearted calls in a negative mood and tell yourself that you've done a day's work.

I know what it is, too, to sit and stare at the wall

and wonder how in the world you're going to pay your bills when you're not doing the job the way you ought to do it. You can't fool me, Brother, it takes one to know one. I've been down that road and I got sick and tired of being poor. I got sick and tired of living in rented houses instead of my own place. I got sick and tired of being dishonest with myself.

Let me tell you what I did one night a few years ago. It was in the middle of a very hot summer and I was sort of flushed financially. I got feeling sorry for myself doing all that hard work and not enjoying myself like some other people were. I got feeling so sorry that I started to sleep late in the morning; at noon I'd take two hours instead of one and along about four o'clock in the afternoon, I started selling myself on the fact that I'd better get back to the hotel and let those poor prospects wait until the next day.

Oh, I did a first-class job of feeling sorry for myself and I started to sell myself on all the reasons why I should take a month's vacation in the North Woods with my family. I almost had myself sold on that course until I had a big, fat truth session with myself one night in a hotel room. I decided to take out my portable typewriter and put down, in writing, just exactly what I wanted to accomplish. All night long I sat in that room and wrote, and when I looked at the results in the morning I decided it was time to get honest with myself and start to do more with my life than just make a living. I decided it was time for me to grow up and start accumulating something.

I decided that the only way I knew how to accomplish this was to get honest with myself and get to work. How the clouds disappear, Brother, when a man finally decides to go to work and make something of himself, and how the money does roll in when you build up a success momentum. When I got through with that little old truth session with myself in that hotel room I did more selling in one month than I'd done in three. You see, I quit fooling myself and good things began to happen on every side. So you're a salesman? Brother, when you tell me that, prove it.

How do you organize your time? Do you have a definite plan to follow when you step out of the door in the morning? If you do, I know you've earned the right to call yourself a salesman, and I know you're not worried about meeting the month's bills but, Brother, if you rock down the road like a tumbleweed hoping to make it big without organization, you're as blind as a cave full of bats. Until you learn to organize your day in writing, don't expect to move out of the corn pone and turnip league. It's just not in the cards.

You can't build anything solid until you first put down a firm foundation. The foundation of great salesmanship is self-honesty. When you can look at yourself in the mirror every day for thirty days and tell yourself that you've really done your best, that you've really gone out there and worked, that you've worked with a plan, that you put in a full day's work every day, you can call yourself a salesman and you can begin to do the things that good salesmen do. You can begin to have the things that good salesmen have. You can hold up your head and be a man and you'll begin to receive the respect and admiration that a real man is entitled to. It's much more fun to be a winner!

My friends, I know I have touched you in a tender spot, but so does the surgeon when he has to operate. Somebody had to operate on you or you might have gone on in the same old rut year after year. Go out and buy yourself a five-cent pencil and a ten-cent notebook and begin to write down some million-dollar ideas for yourself. Write down exactly what you want and what you intend to give for it. Then get out and go to work as you've never worked before. A month from today when somebody says, so you're a salesman, you can answer: *You bet I am!*

———————————————

Selling is a mental process in which you, as a salesman, should control your own reactions and endeavor to deliberately affect the feeling, emotion, instincts and reason of your prospect for the purpose of creating a desire within him sufficiently strong to motivate him to act in the direction you desire—and thus complete a sale.

LEARN TO CONTROL REACTIONS

by W. CLEMENT STONE

You and your prospect are each individuals who act and react, in many respects, like two magnets. Each affects, and is affected by, external forces, including each other. A like force repels like in proportion *to the direction* of the opposing force. Like forces attract, unite, work together with like and accentuate the strength of their powers when they are directly in line and *headed in the same direction*.

Get your current of thought and that of your prospect in line and united so that your two minds pull together and push *in the same direction*, rather than oppose each other. The speed of an electric motor or the power of a generator is the result of the control of the reaction or the attraction and repulsion of opposite and like magnetic poles.

As a salesman, you think you are a pretty fine person, don't you? (Don't sell yourself short—of course you are.) Then why is it that some individuals cause an unfavorable reaction within you and some prospects react unfavorably toward you? What can you do about it?

Control your own reactions. Develop the desire to truly understand yourself! When this is done, do something about it. You have inherited the capacity to control your own mind; therefore, you can control your mental attitudes. Be prepared! Use reason to develop a wholesome, positive, optimistic outlook. Train yourself to respond immediately in action when you use slogans, words or signs to neutralize or change the direction of your thoughts, feelings and emotions. You will then find that you can control your own reactions during the emotional strain of a sale.

If you take the time to develop the habit of controlling your own reactions, you will instinctively sense the signals and employ the principles in controlling the reactions of others.

A powerful, young emotional type of salesman called on the owner of a shoe store in Chicago Heights, Illinois. When the owner of the store indicated that he wasn't interested, the salesman, who had been trying desperately to make a sale in front of his sales manager, exploded in anger, "I would never come to your store to buy a pair of shoes!"

This salesman allowed an external force to cause an undesirable reaction within him—he was not prepared. When you are turned down, do you act unhappy?

This salesman was so emotionally upset that he didn't make a sale until his sales manager pointed

out that the prospect gave his time for which the salesman should be grateful and that, if he would leave each
place of business making the prospect feel good and
happy even though he had refused him, the salesman
would himself be in a friendly, happy frame of mind
and thus be in a position to direct the next prospect's
thinking in the proper channel. The sales manager then
demonstrated and proved the effectiveness of controlled
reaction by making several sales.

When you are selling, do your feelings get hurt
easily? If they do, you are the person who frequently
hurts the feelings of others. Your own negative thoughts
cause an intensified negative force by changing the
direction of your prospects' thinking in line with your
own negative attitude. If your feelings are very seldom
or never hurt, then your positive, optimistic thinking
and depth of understanding of the feelings of others
will control their reaction *in the same direction.*

Control your prospect's reactions. To control the
reaction of your prospect, be sensitive and alert to all
the indications of his feelings, emotions, instinctive
tendencies and reason. Unpleasantries are experienced
by the salesman who appeals to reason alone and is
not sensitive to the feelings of others. Lose the argument, but win the sale. Push in the *right direction*—
don't "rub the wrong way"! Change *direction* so that
like attracts like!

When your prospect makes a statement or asks a
question, his statement or question can, if you are
alerted to signals, indicate his trend of thought. He
gives you a cue as to *the direction* of his thinking.
(What good is a cue to an actor or a salesman if he
is not prepared to respond?) Observe and catch
signals indicating this reaction so that you can immediately stimulate and direct a new response, as well

as anticipate and forestall unfavorable ideas or actions that might otherwise be *misdirected*.

Your push your prospect's thinking *in a negative direction* and away from a sale if you talk on unpleasant subjects, such as your sore tooth, your sicknesses, your complaints about others' jealousies and unkind acts toward you, dishonesty or unfairness of others toward you, bad weather, hard times, hard luck, etc.

Your prospect is not interested in your troubles; therefore, he will dislike being with you. If he does listen, he will probably give you the satisfaction of experiencing more "hard luck" so that you can continue to think in the same pessimistic *direction* that has its own reward—defeat.

By stimulating as many of the five senses of your prospect as possible, you accentuate your *control of the direction* of the sale. You stimulate his imagination with descriptive words, phrases, pictures, etc.

The first time you look at a menu in one of the Toffenetti Restaurants in Chicago or New York, you *see* a colorful picture of "OLD-FASHIONED STRAWBERRY SHORTCAKE WITH FRESH WHIPPED CREAM," and your imagination is stimulated with "Following the trail of the summer sun, we discover and rediscover new and more wonderful strawberries. California comes to the front again with the most luscious strawberries. The way they're fixed at Toffenetti's it makes a shortcake superlative." You *hear* the sizzle of the "TANTALIZING, TENDERIZED, JUICY, THICK, BONELESS, CLUB STEAK SERVED WITH FRENCH ONIONS, AMERICAN FRIED POTATOES AND A BOWL OF CHEF'S SALAD." You *smell* the hickory when you read "Our hams are zealously guarded from the cares of the world so their meat will always be tender and finely grained. These hams are cured in smarting brine, Hickory Smoked and in our kitchen are roasted through and through to a marvelous tenderness which you will love and make you wish for more." And your sense of *touch* and *taste* are stimulated with "There is nothing like it to compare: The tantalizing mildness, succulent juiciness and the tempting fragrance and sugar roasting—plus the way it's served with those gorgeous sweet potatoes and refreshing cole slaw that will make your heart tingle as you behold an order of HAM 'N SWEETS!"

LEARN TO CONTROL REACTION—get your prospect in line and *headed in the same direction!*

No salesman ever became great until he mastered his fear of that unseen prospect behind the door.

OPEN THAT CLOSED DOOR— AND SELL

by N. C. CHRISTENSEN

Eager to pick up ideas that would boost our sales and increase our income, we hurried to the conference room. The speaker was a veteran salesman with an annual income in the five-figure class. This is what he told us:

"Whenever your hand reaches out to open a prospect's door, keep this in mind: Behind that door may be a selfish person. The odds are that he or she is dominated by self-interest. If you want to cash in on this call, you've got to appeal to your prospect's streak of selfishness, no matter how well concealed it may be."

Discouraging?

No!

Challenging?

Yes!

It is this intriguing element of human relations that makes selling so fascinating.

"You'll never know what's behind a closed door," another professional salesman told me, "until you open it."

But now that you have opened the door and you face the prospect you recall what the speaker told you about this prospect. "He's probably selfish," we were told. So to appeal to his streak of selfishness is your immediate and challenging problem.

One of the most successful specialty-advertising salesmen I have ever known declared he had never sold a calendar, had never sold a ball-point pen, had never sold a mailing piece or any other item in his vast line. "I built up my sales record by selling the power of these media to get more business, more profits for my customers. I never sold the item itself as a piece of merchandise."

Since then I learned by experience that the positive approach is the key to successful selling whether your line is advertising, real estate, automobiles, shoes or any other product or service.

And speaking of shoes, a salesman recently came to my office and placed a custom-made shoe in my hands suggesting that I feel the softness of the leather, the smoothness of the lining, the scientific contour of the built-in arch support. He pointed out features of that shoe that would lift the burden from my feet, that would give me comfort and that would also give me pride in wearing it. He never let up on the comfort theme. Again and again he appealed to my self-interest.

Yes, I bought the shoes. I wanted my feet to feel happy again. I wanted to enjoy comfort and he had sold foot comfort to me, not just shoes.

An automobile salesman I know consistently outdistances other salesmen in his firm in the race for total volume. I heard him making his sales talk to a well-dressed, middle-aged couple on the display floor. Did he sell nuts and bolts and everlasting steel construction? He did not. He sold styling, beauty, luxury, comfort, power and prestige. He insisted on the lady getting into the driver's seat. Her face lit up as she took the wheel in her hands. He urged her to feel the soft quality of the upholstery. He got her to commit herself on color preference. And her husband? He concurred. When he saw the approving smile his wife gave him, he made a cursory under-the-hood inspection; then he was ready to work out the closing details.

On a shopping tour one evening I trailed my wife into the beauty salon in a large department store. Did the "counselor" who greeted my wife sell her complexion creams and skin lotions? Not that astute young saleslady. She talked about results only. She told my wife how consistent use of her "recommended" complexion cream would "preserve" the youthful, wrinkle-free smoothness of her skin. To support her claims for her product she presented "certified" endorsements from women who had experienced "marvelous results" even with "obstinate skin problems."

Clinching this sale was merely a beginning for this experienced sales person. She then "introduced" to my wife "something that has just been released after years of laboratory testing"—a new skin lotion. She suggested my wife rub some of the lotion on her hands.

"Please notice how refreshing this lotion is," she said, feeling my wife's hand. "Just notice how your skin drinks in this lotion, how soft your skin begins to feel. Doesn't it have a delightful aroma, too? I am sure once you've tried this lotion you'll never be without it."

In that enlightening demonstration I had witnessed professional selling in action. The whole appeal was to a woman's self-interest and to her vanity—feminine beauty, wrinkle-free complexion, smooth hands, preservation of the youthful look.

Whether the prospect is male or female, the appeal to the selfish streak usually is effective. We need only to make our bid to his or her self-interest and we get immediate attention. We hold that attention by drumming away on how our prospect can profit by buying what we have to sell. And by profit we do not always mean money. We may mean comfort, pride, good looks, good health, beauty or perhaps prestige.

We appeal to pride and vanity when we suggest that trees and shrubs we have for sale could well make our prospect's yard the envy of his neighbors.

We appeal to pride and to vanity when we suggest to a nurse that wearing our uniforms will win for her the envy of other nurses and the admiration of patients and doctors because of her stunning professional appearance.

A salesman demonstrating a fireprotecting device for the home touched a tender spot in his prospect's makeup to bring out deep response by arousing his self-interest. He had made his presentation but the prospect still hesitated. The salesman closed the sale by switching his appeal to concern for the safety of his prospect's family.

"For the sake of those you love, can you think of a better investment than protection like this from fire?" he asked. "Really, it costs so little when the lives of your family are at stake. Why risk another day without this protection for them?"

There are many angles to the self-interest appeal that can be used effectively. Of course, they call for creative thinking and a positive attitude, but that is why selling is so interesting. All successful salesmen know that we do not barge in and dump our samples on our prospect's table or desk and say: "There you have it. Take your choice." We try to be more imaginative than that.

Our approach, to be effective, requires thought, planning and skill. We learn by experience to stay on the track and not to be led into blind alleys. We try to keep our prospects on the track, too, because we hope the track we are on will lead to a sale.

One aggressive sales manager under whom I worked and learned gave me this tip:

"When you open your sales talk, drive straight for a close. Don't wander. Try to follow a step-by-step presentation for reaching your target, which is the sale of your product or service.

"When you meet your prospect," he said, "make your inroduction warm, friendly but brief. Then get attention fastened on what you have to sell by showing what your product or service will do for him. That's the sure-fire appeal. It is the approach used by insurance salesmen who come up with top records. It is the persuasive appeal used by successful advertising salesmen. It is an effective attention getter and action promoter with either business people or those whose primary interest is the home."

The veteran "pro" who told us that our prospects probably would be selfish people also gave us this sage advice.

"Hammer away on benefits to your prospect. Don't let up. Get your prospect to agree with you often on those benefits. Each time you win his or her agreement, you are one step nearer to a smooth close and a sale."

In my own selling experience I discovered that an approach to closing a sale may be technically correct and yet miss the target. I learned that my "misses" and "near misses" frequently lacked one important ingredient—my own enthusiasm.

Are you thoroughly sold on what you are selling?

Do you sincerely believe your product or service will do for your prospect what you claim it will do?

I learned by the tough trial-and-error method that when I was weak in my own conviction my sales talk fell flat. I didn't ring true. I failed to make the sale. Why? Because subconsciously I was nursing the same doubts that influenced my prospect. So I made up my mind to first sell my line to myself before tackling any prospects in their dens. And it paid off!

To sell the man (or woman) behind the door, get all fired up on the possibilities of your line, on the benefits it promises to your customers. Then with the sincerity and enthusiasm of an evangelist go out after sales. The odds then will be with you to win.

If you are a salesman and want to be a sales manager, you have your opportunity—now. You can start immediately. How? Begin to manage yourself! I dare you to try it. Whether you now are, or intend to become, a sales manager of a small, medium, large or enormous sales organization, you can be assured of success in any sales management responsibility if you are first able to manage yourself. Regardless of your title, if you are a person who is fortunate enough to have the responsibility of sales management at any level, with an organization of any size, be a sales manager in act as well as name.

HOW TO BECOME A
SALES MANAGER—NOW!

by W. CLEMENT STONE

The three ingredients necessary for the success of a salesman or sales manager are technical knowledge of his product or service, know-how of specific sales techniques successfully to merchandise that product or service, and inspiration to action. A sales manager who possesses these three ingredients is in a position to demonstrate what he preaches and thereby to inspire his representatives to have faith in him and to "go and do likewise."

Some sales managers can sell more merchandise in a given day than any salesman in the United States, or at least so it seems at a sales meeting. But they are actually miserable failures in the field. Thus they cannot instruct the salesmen under their supervision in the art of being successful in their particular business. These men are sales managers in name only, and that not for long. To be a sales manager in act as well as name, the successful sales manager employs the three ingredients in the following manner:

1. *He studies!* In order to have new seeds of thought which, when employed, can ripen into the harvest, he studies at least one inspirational book on self-improvement every year, and preferably one each quarter.

2. *He plans!* He follows the example of those who have become great and engages in thinking time. He uses the working tools of an Albert Einstein— a pencil and a pad of paper—and jots down the ideas and plans which occur to him in this thinking and planning time. *He plans his work so that he can work his plan!*

3. *He organizes!* A frugal housewife will go from store to store to save a penny or two on each item. Anyone who deals with the public knows that quality with price appeal will bring sales. Get organized! Increase your efficiency, capacity, sales and profits—by saving time. Where do you start? Start with yourself right where you are! When? *Do it now!* If you organize your time, you will find that often you will be able in one hour to do the work of ten. Because he and his army were well organized, Napoleon correctly calculated that one of his soldiers was equivalent to six of the enemy.

4. *He controls* himself and his men. A sales manager must direct those under his supervision so that planned-for results are achieved. The standard measurement used in evaluating success is: *Results*

are what count! (This statement is to be interpreted
in the light of the highest ethical standards. We do
not mean that unethical means are justified if satisfactory sales results are obtained. It is understood
that no results are satisfactory results if they have
been achieved through unethical procedures.)

An outstandingly successful sales manager habit-
ually lives the Golden Rule. He deals with other
persons as he would have them deal with him. And
because of his example, the salesmen under his supervision come to understand the value of ethical behavior
and raise their own standards to meet the level of the
sales manager.

5. *He makes decisions!* You, as a present or future
sales manager, will need to develop the habit of
coming to logical decisions after evaluating known
factors and reckoning with those which may be unknown. This habit can be developed very easily,
and the results will be most beneficial.

What if you make a wrong decision? Say to yourself, "That's good!" Then ask yourself, "What's good
about it? How can I turn this unexpected result into
a seed of an equivalent benefit? How can I capitalize
on it?" If you will adopt this practice, you will find
that all of your decisions eventually turn out to be
good decisions. Why? Because you will make them so.

6. *He communicates!* In an organization, large or
small, proper communication between parties involved is imperative for an efficient, successful
operation. Keep in mind that what may be logical
to you in view of your background, experience and
knowledge of a given situation is not necessarily
logical or known to someone else.

A youngster accepted a job in a grocery store. He
was a willing worker. In fact, he invested $3.75 for
his first pair of long trousers just to get the job. But

the boss fired him after fifteen minutes of work. Why? The boy had been asked to weigh potatoes on a balance scale and had done it incorrectly. The owner probably had a fit when he saw the boy place the potatoes in the bag after the scalepan had fallen lower than the one carrying the balance weight. But the owner had not instructed the boy on the use of the scale. Poor communications! That which was known and logical to the store owner was not known, and had not been offered, to the inexperienced lad.

7. *He leads!* Don't sell yourself short. You can be a great sales leader of any size organization, even though you weren't a football hero, an officer of one or more clubs or are not now a backslapping, happy-go-lucky, hard-drinking extrovert. The only requirements for successful sales leadership are the three ingredients to success mentioned above, properly employed.

The field of sales management is so vast, and the need so great, that there are jobs for every personality: aggressive or timid, extroverted or introverted, contented, dependent or independent. You fit somewhere in these categories, don't you? To succeed you employ the three ingredients to success—and surround yourself with individuals who have the characteristics you lack when they are needed.

8. *He delegates!* To delegate successfully, you must be willing to accept certain fundamental concepts: 1) You must sincerely want to delegate certain responsibilities. 2) Be ready to accept the fact that your choice of individuals may at times be wrong. 3) Be willing to recognize the fact that perhaps someone else can do a part of your job better than you can. 4) Accept the fact that some errors will be made by the delegate, particularly during the training period. 5) Be willing to measure job per-

formance by methods employed as well as results achieved. 6) Be prepared to disclose intimate knowledge of the job that is being delegated. 7) Be willing to put a person into a job before he is fully prepared so that he can gain the experience necessary to develop competence. 8) Be willing to delegate a "whole" job.

If you are willing sincerely to subscribe to these concepts, then the following additional action will be necessary:

1. Establish the responsibility of the delegate by making sure that he understands just what results you expect of him.

2. Give him the authority he requires to do the job by having him understand thoroughly just what he may or may not do in order to accomplish the desired results.

3. Establish accountability by having him understand what methods will be used to measure his success or failure.

Be a Sales Manager in *act* as well **as** name!

ABOUT THE AUTHORS

ASHLEY, NOVA TRIMBLE. A prize-winning Kansas author of many poems, short stories and articles. She is a member of the Kansas Press Women, National Federation of Press Women and the Kansas Authors' Club.

BRADLEY, DR. PRESTON D. The author of nine books including two best sellers, *Courage for Today* and *Mastering Fear*, he has been pastor of the Peoples Church of Chicago for fifty-four years and his lectures and addresses are world-famous.

BINSTOCK, DR. LOUIS. Rabbi of Temple Sholom in Chicago. His writings have appeared in numerous periodicals, and he is the author of two outstanding books in the inspirational and self-help field, *The Power of Faith* and *The Road to Successful Living*.

CASEWIT, CURTIS W. Besides two books on his specialty, skiing, and another on *How to Get a Job Overseas*, this member of the Society of Magazine Writers has seen his work appear in *Parade, Cosmopolitan, Coronet, This Day, Saga, Today's Family* and *Rotarian*.

CHRISTENSEN, N. C. Now retired from the advertising agency field, he writes with the authority and experience of over twenty-five years in newspaper work, including positions as executive editor of the Associated Press in Cleveland and Columbus, Ohio, plus over ten years as a sales and marketing executive.

COX, CLAIRE. She is the author of five books, including *How Women Can Make up to $1,000 a Week in Direct Selling* and *How to Beat the High Cost of College.* Her articles have appeared in *Good Housekeeping, Seventeen, Dare* and *Pageant.*

DEWEY, EDWARD R. Executive director of the Foundation for the Study of Cycles and co-author of the best seller *Cycles: The Science of Prediction.* He has written extensively for magazines and scientific journals.

DUBOIS, CLEO GEHRKE. Her horticultural articles have appeared in *Better Homes and Gardens, Flower and Garden, Flower Grower* and *American Home.* She now writes almost exclusively in the inspirational field.

FERGUSON, HENRY N. Assistant general manager of the Port of Brownsville, Texas, he turned to free-lance writing and has sold more than a thousand articles to some two hundred magazines in the past ten years.

GOOD, R. M. President emeritus, School of the Ozarks, Point Lookout, Missouri. His articles have also appeared in *Rotary* and *Guideposts.*

GRINDE, ROBERT A. His dynamic voice and hard-hitting ideas influenced and inspired thousands of persons on radio, records and in speeches.

HILL, NAPOLEON. Author of one of the greatest bestsellers of all time, *Think and Grow Rich* (Hawthorn), five other books, and inspirational self-help articles which are a regular feature of *Success Unlimited* magazine.

HUBBARD, KELLEY. A California housewife and mother of two daughters, she has written articles for *Bon Appétit, The Record, Parents' Magazine, Pen, Minutes* and *National Motorist.*

JENKINS, JEWEL MARET. Now retired to "town" after a life on the plains of eastern Colorado, she has written for *Home Life, Capper's Weekly, The Christian, Empire* magazine and the *American Swedish Monthly.*

LENNON, LILA. A former Chicago *Tribune* columnist and radio personality, her features, fiction and poetry have appeared in national magazines. She was the recipient of the 1959 Open Door Award for her individual contribution to the public understanding of the problems of alcoholism.

LURTON, DOUGLAS. The author of numerous books in the motivational field, among them *Make the Most of Your Life, The Power of Positive Living* and *The Complete Home Book of Money-Making Ideas.*

MANDINO, OG. He spent nearly seventeen years in the field as salesman and sales manager before turning his talents to advertising and sales promotion, and is now executive editor of *Success Unlimited. A Treasury of Success Unlimited* is his first anthology.

MCDERMOTT, IRENE. Her articles and fiction have been published in *The Ladies' Home Journal, The Sign, Household, Family Circle* and the *New York Daily News.*

MENNINGER, DR. WILLIAM C. He holds a pre-eminent position in the field of psychiatry. Among his many published works are *Psychiatry in a Troubled World*, *You and Psychiatry* (with Munro Leaf) and *Psychiatry: Its Evolution and Present Status*. He is president of the famous Menninger Foundation in Topeka, Kansas.

MEYER, JACK. Her real name is Irma but a disgusted older brother hung "Jack" on her after she became his seventh sister. She has published stories and articles on a variety of subjects and does her writing after a busy day as a laboratory and X-ray technician.

NEAGLE, MARJORIE SPILLER. She worked as a library assistant until her children completed college and is now teaching creative writing and preparing a novel for publication. She has been published in more than twenty magazines and in an anthology, *The Down East Reader*.

NELSON, BILL. Assistant City Editor of the *Cedar Rapids* (Iowa) *Gazette*. The articles of this former marine have appeared in *Ford Times*, *Guideposts*, *Christian Science Monitor*, *The Lutheran* and *Sunday Digest*.

PEALE, DR. NORMAN VINCENT. Pastor of America's oldest Protestant institution, New York's Marble Collegiate Church, he has published such best-sellers as *The Power of Positive Thinking*, *A Guide to Confident Living* and *Sin, Sex and Self-Control*. His articles appear regularly in *Success Unlimited* and he is also editor-in-chief of *Guideposts* magazine.

PROUTY, RALPH E. A teacher of English at Willoughby North High School near Cleveland, Ohio, he has sold over 50 articles since he began writing professionally a few years ago.

REMINGTON, FRANK L. A free-lance writer since 1952, he has been published in over two hundred magazines.

ROPER, WILLIAM L. He first became interested in positive thinking during a summer vacation in 1916 when he earned his college tuition selling Orison S. Marden's famous self-help book, *Pushing to the Front.* He is a retired newspaperman and his articles have been published in more than a hundred magazines in the United States and England.

ROSE, FRANK. A former columnist for the Fort Lauderdale *News,* his articles have appeared in the *Reader's Digest, Redbook, Coronet, Mechanix Illustrated, Ford Times, Family Weekly,* and the *Wall Street Journal.*

SAINSBURY, ED. Midwest sports editor for United Press International since 1946, he has lost count of the number of articles and published stories that have appeared under his byline and for the news wires. He claims his proudest accomplishment must be shared with Mrs. Sainsbury—eight wonderful children.

SCHUSTER, M. LINCOLN. Co-founder, former president and editor in chief, Simon and Schuster, Inc. Among his previous publications are *A Treasury of the World's Great Letters: From Ancient Times to Our Own Time* and *Eyes on the World: A Photographic Record of History in the Making.*

SHERMAN, HAROLD. President and Executive Director of the ESP Research Associates Foundation. He is the author of countless articles and books on the power of the mind. Among them are *The New TNT: Miraculous Power Within You, How to Solve Mysteries of Your Mind and Soul* and *How to Use the Power of Prayer.*

SPAULDING, JAMES C. The Milwaukee *Journal's* reporter on medicine for fourteen years, covering major developments in the health field. He writes a weekly feature of general interest, "Report on Your Health," and contributes articles on health to many magazines.

STONE, W. CLEMENT. Editor and Publisher, *Success Unlimited* magazine, president of the Combined Group of Companies, author of *The Success System That Never Fails* and co-author of *Success Through a Positive Mental Attitude* and *The Other Side of the Mind.* His editorials and sales articles are a monthly feature of *Success Unlimited* magazine.

STOWELL, EARL. Engineering publications director for AiResearch Mfg. Co. in California, his feature articles have been in *Family Circle, American Business, Boys' Life, Popular Electronics,* and *QST.* His latest book is entitled *The Magic of Mormonism.*

SWEETLAND, BEN. Two of his books, *I Can* and *I Will,* have sold in the millions. He was a dynamic teacher, radio and TV personality, and his classes on creative psychology are still remembered fondly by those who attended. Another of his books, *Grow Rich While You Sleep,* has been translated into Japanese.

TETZLAFF, RAYMOND A. In 1963, he took an aptitude test and was told he was wasting his time as a factory manager and should be writing. Since then he has sold hundreds of feature stories and photos to over thirty periodicals, including the *Christian Science Monitor* and the Milwaukee *Journal*.

VALENTRY, DUANE. A full-time author for nearly twenty years, she has written articles for *Good Business, Science Digest, Western Horseman, Dodge News, Lion* and *Rotarian*. She is also a composer and singer.

VRETTOS, THEODORE. A former teacher of English and creative writing at Northeastern University and at the Boston Center, he is now devoting all his time to writing. His first novel, *Hammer on the Sea,* has recently been published.

WALKER, DR. HAROLD BLAKE. Senior minister, First Presbyterian Church, Evanston, Illinois. His books include *Going God's Way, Ladder of Light, Upper Room on Main Street, Power to Manage Yourself* and *Thoughts to Live By*. His articles appear frequently in *Success Unlimited*.

WELLMAN, ALICE. Former assistant director in film production after an earlier career in musical comedy and operettas, she now concentrates her creative interest on writing. She is the author of many nonfiction and fiction pieces as well as a novel for teen-agers.